*maranGraphics™ Learn at First Sight™*

# WordPerfect® 6.0 for Wind

**maranGraphics' Development Group**

**Published in the United States**
**by Prentice Hall, Inc.**
**Englewood Cliffs, New Jersey, 07632**

Telephone: 1-800-223-1360
Fax: 1-800-445-6991

**Distributed in Canada**
**by Prentice Hall Canada**

Telephone: 1-800-567-3800
Fax: 416-299-2529

**Distributed Internationally**
**by Simon & Schuster**

Telephone: 201-767-4990
Fax: 201-767-5625

**SINGLE COPY PURCHASES (U.S.)**

Telephone: 515-284-6751
Fax: 515-284-2607

*maranGraphics*™ ***Learn at First Sight***™
***WordPerfect*** ® ***6.0 for Windows***™

## Trademark Acknowledgments

Published by Prentice Hall, Inc.
A Paramount Publishing Company
Englewood Cliffs, New Jersey 07632

maranGraphics Inc. has attempted to include trademark information for products, services and companies referred to in this guide. Although maranGraphics Inc. has made reasonable efforts in gathering this information, it cannot guarantee its accuracy.
WordPerfect®.

WordPerfect is a registered trademark of WordPerfect Corporation within the United States and other countries.

Grammatik and WPCorp are registered trademarks of WordPerfect Corporation within the United States and other countries.

Button Bar is a trademark of WordPerfect Corporation worldwide.

Microsoft, MS-DOS and Microsoft Mouse are registered trademarks and Windows is a trademark of Microsoft Corporation.

The animated characters are the copyright of maranGraphics, Inc.

Printed in the United States of America

10      9      8      7      6      5      4      3      2      1

**Author:**
    Ruth Maran

**Art Director – Cover
Design and Layout:**
    Jim C. Leung

**Illustrator and Screens:**
    Dave Ross

**Screens:**
    Béla Korcsog

**Technical Consultant:**
    Wendi Blouin Ewbank

**Proofreading:**
    Judy Maran
    Monica Walraven

# Acknowledgments

Special thanks to Wendi B. Ewbank for ensuring the technical accuracy of this book.

To the dedicated staff of maranGraphics including Mia P. Chao, Saulina DeFrias, David Hendricks, Béla Korcsog, Jim C. Leung, Judy Maran, Maxine Maran, Robert Maran, Dave Ross and Monica Walraven.

And finally, to Richard Maran who originated the easy-to-use graphic format of this guide. Thank you for your inspiration and guidance.

# Table of Contents

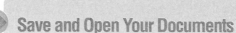

**Introduction**
Mouse Basics
Start WordPerfect
Enter Text
The WordPerfect Buttons

Using the Menus
Move Through a Document
Select Text
Help

## What You Can Create With WordPerfect for Windows

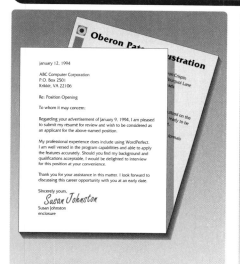

### PERSONAL AND BUSINESS LETTERS

WordPerfect for Windows helps you to produce letters quickly and accurately.

### MAILING LISTS

WordPerfect for Windows can merge documents with a list of names and addresses to produce personalized letters.

### REPORTS AND MANUALS

WordPerfect for Windows provides editing and formatting features that make it ideal for producing longer documents such as reports and manuals.

Let's Assume...

◆ You have installed the WordPerfect for Windows program on your hard drive.

◆ You are using a mouse with WordPerfect for Windows.

# MOUSE BASICS

The mouse enables you to quickly select commands and perform actions.

## Using the Mouse

Hold the mouse as shown in the diagram. Use your thumb and two rightmost fingers to guide the mouse while your two remaining fingers press the mouse buttons.

## Moving the Mouse Pointer

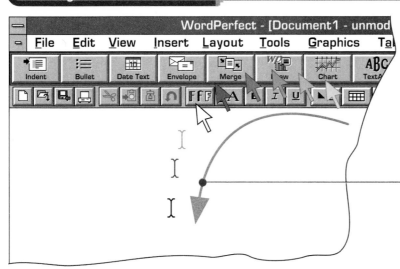

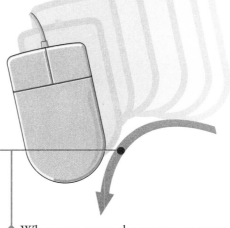

◆ When you move the mouse on your desk, the mouse pointer ($\&$ or $I$) on your screen also moves. The mouse pointer changes shape depending on its location on your screen.

◇ The mouse has a left and right button. You can use these buttons to:

- open menus
- select commands
- choose options

*Note: You will use the left button most of the time.*

◆ Under the mouse is a ball that senses movement. To ensure smooth motion of the mouse, you should occasionally remove and clean this ball.

## Mouse Terms

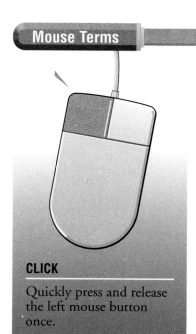

### CLICK

Quickly press and release the left mouse button once.

### DOUBLE-CLICK

Quickly press and release the left mouse button twice.

### DRAG

When the mouse pointer ( ▸ or I ) is over an object on your screen, press and hold down the left mouse button and then move the mouse.

When you start WordPerfect for Windows, a blank document appears. You can now begin to type text into this document.

## Start WordPerfect for Windows

`C:\> WIN_`

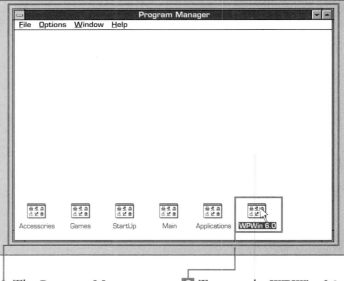

**1** To start WordPerfect for Windows from MS-DOS, type **WIN** and then press Enter .

◆ The **Program Manager** window appears.

**2** To open the **WPWin 6.0** group window, move the mouse over its icon and then quickly press the left button twice.

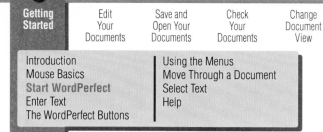

| Getting Started | Edit Your Documents | Save and Open Your Documents | Check Your Documents | Change Document View | Format Your Documents | Create a Table | Print Your Documents | Use Multiple Documents | Using Graphics | Merge Documents |

Introduction
Mouse Basics
**Start WordPerfect**
Enter Text
The WordPerfect Buttons

Using the Menus
Move Through a Document
Select Text
Help

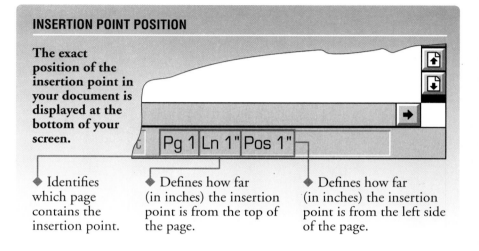

## INSERTION POINT POSITION

**The exact position of the insertion point in your document is displayed at the bottom of your screen.**

Pg 1 Ln 1" Pos 1"

◆ Identifies which page contains the insertion point.

◆ Defines how far (in inches) the insertion point is from the top of the page.

◆ Defines how far (in inches) the insertion point is from the left side of the page.

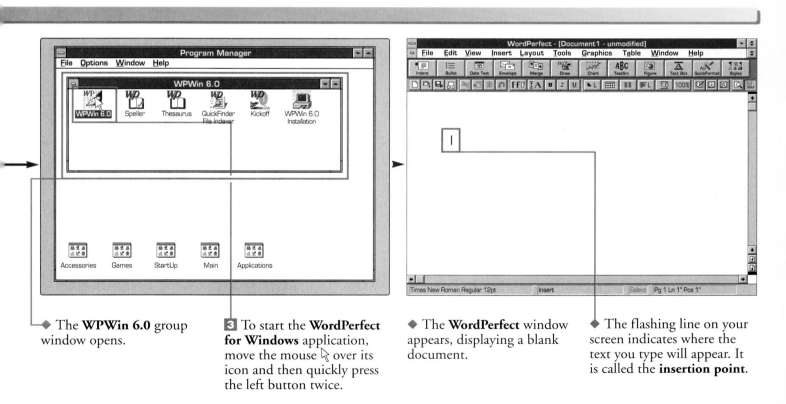

◆ The **WPWin 6.0** group window opens.

**3** To start the **WordPerfect for Windows** application, move the mouse ⬚ over its icon and then quickly press the left button twice.

◆ The **WordPerfect** window appears, displaying a blank document.

◆ The flashing line on your screen indicates where the text you type will appear. It is called the **insertion point**.

When typing text in your document, you do not need to press **Enter** at the end of a line. WordPerfect automatically moves the text to the next line. This is called word wrapping.

When using a word processor to type a letter, the text au...

When using a word processor to type a letter, the text automatically wraps to the next line as you type.

## Enter Text

### IMPORTANT!

◆ To display the examples in this guide more clearly, the design and size of the text were changed.

*Note: To change the design and size of text, refer to page 66.*

| Initial or default font | New font |
|---|---|
| Times New Roman 12 point ► | Arial 16 point |

◆ To work faster in WordPerfect, display your document in the Draft mode.

*Note: To change modes, refer to page 54.*

---

WordPerfect - [Document1]

File   Edit   View   Insert   Layout   Tools   Graphics   Table

Indent   Bullet   Date Text   Envelope   Merge   Draw   Chart   TextArt

Dear Mr. Linton:

---

◆ The flashing line on your screen indicates where the text you type will appear. It is called the **insertion point**.

**1** Type the first line of text.

**2** To start a new paragraph, press **Enter** twice.

The WordPerfect buttons enable you to quickly select commonly used commands.

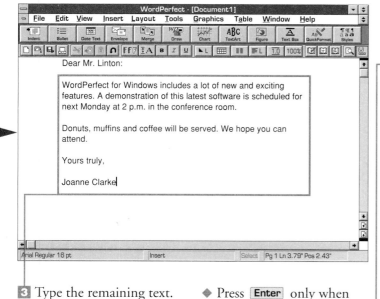

## The WordPerfect Buttons

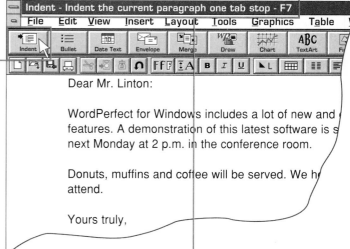

**3** Type the remaining text.

◆ Press **Enter** only when you want to start a new line or paragraph.

**You can display a description of any button displayed on your screen.**

**1** Move the mouse ⍐ over the button of interest (example: **Indent**).

◆ A description of the button appears at the top of your screen.

# USING THE MENUS

You can open a menu to display a list of related commands. You can then select the command you want to use.

## Using the Menus

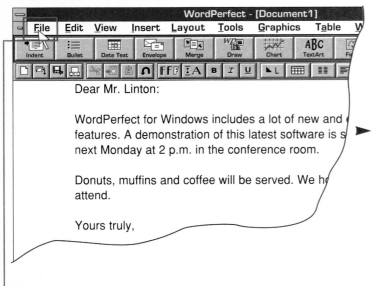

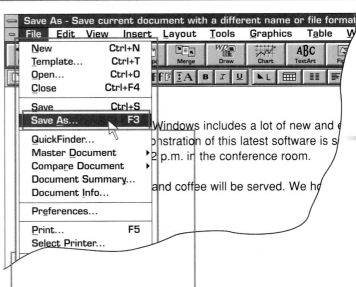

**1** To open a menu, move the mouse ↳ over the menu name (example: **File**) and then press the left button.

◆ A menu appears displaying a list of related commands.

*Note: To close a menu, move the mouse I anywhere over your document and then press the left button.*

**2** To select a command, move the mouse ↳ over the command name (example: **Save As**) and then press the left button.

Introduction
Mouse Basics
Start WordPerfect
Enter Text
The WordPerfect Buttons

**Using the Menus**
Move Through a Document
Select Text
Help

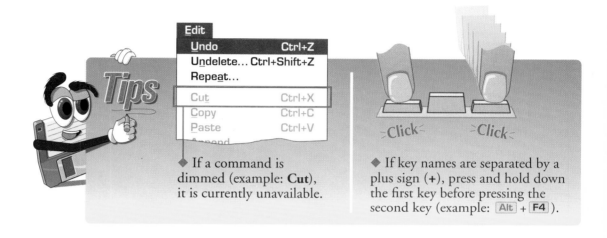

◆ If a command is dimmed (example: **Cut**), it is currently unavailable.

◆ If key names are separated by a plus sign (+), press and hold down the first key before pressing the second key (example: Alt + F4 ).

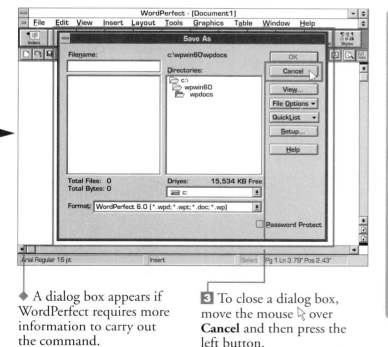

◆ A dialog box appears if WordPerfect requires more information to carry out the command.

**3** To close a dialog box, move the mouse ↕ over **Cancel** and then press the left button.

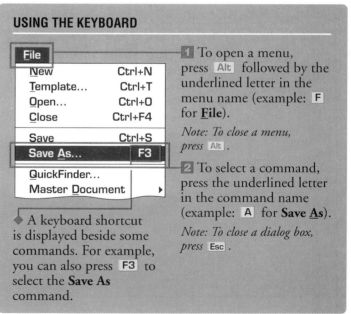

## USING THE KEYBOARD

**1** To open a menu, press Alt followed by the underlined letter in the menu name (example: F for **File**).

*Note: To close a menu, press Alt .*

**2** To select a command, press the underlined letter in the command name (example: A for **Save As**).

*Note: To close a dialog box, press Esc .*

◆ A keyboard shortcut is displayed beside some commands. For example, you can also press F3 to select the **Save As** command.

# MOVE THROUGH A DOCUMENT

> You can use the mouse or the keyboard to move through your document.

## Move to Any Position on Your Screen

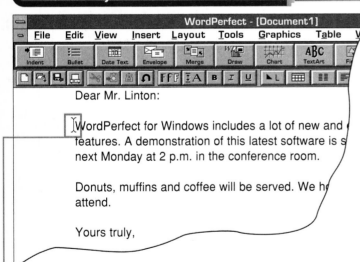

**1** Move the mouse I over the location where you want to position the insertion point and then press the left button.

## KEYBOARD SHORTCUTS

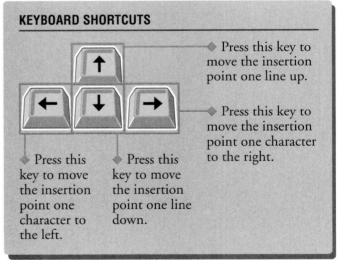

◆ Press this key to move the insertion point one line up.

◆ Press this key to move the insertion point one character to the right.

◆ Press this key to move the insertion point one character to the left.

◆ Press this key to move the insertion point one line down.

| Getting Started | Edit Your Documents | Save and Open Your Documents | Check Your Documents | Change Document View | Format Your Documents | Create a Table | Print Your Documents | Use Multiple Documents | Using Graphics | Merge Documents |
|---|---|---|---|---|---|---|---|---|---|---|

Introduction
Mouse Basics
Start WordPerfect
Enter Text
The WordPerfect Buttons

Using the Menus
**Move Through a Document**
Select Text
Help

## Scroll Up or Down

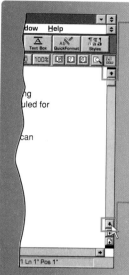

◆ To scroll up one line, move the mouse ⌖ over the up arrow ⬆ and then press the left button.

*Note: You can use the scroll arrows and scroll bar to view information that extends beyond one screen **or** when your document is displayed in the Page mode. To change modes, refer to page 54.*

◆ To scroll down one line, move the mouse ⌖ over the down arrow ⬇ and then press the left button.

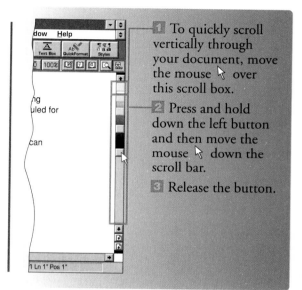

**1** To quickly scroll vertically through your document, move the mouse ⌖ over this scroll box.

**2** Press and hold down the left button and then move the mouse ⌖ down the scroll bar.

**3** Release the button.

## View Previous or Next Page

**If your document contains more than one page, you can view the previous or next page.**

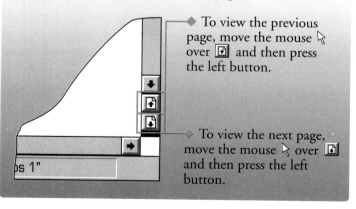

◆ To view the previous page, move the mouse ⌖ over 🔼 and then press the left button.

◆ To view the next page, move the mouse ⌖ over 🔽 and then press the left button.

### KEYBOARD SHORTCUTS

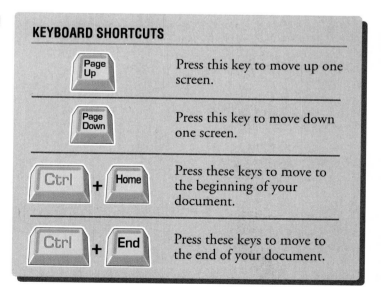

Press this key to move up one screen. *(Page Up)*

Press this key to move down one screen. *(Page Down)*

Press these keys to move to the beginning of your document. *(Ctrl + Home)*

Press these keys to move to the end of your document. *(Ctrl + End)*

Before you can use many WordPerfect features, you must first select the text you want to change. Selected text appears highlighted on your screen.

## Select a Word

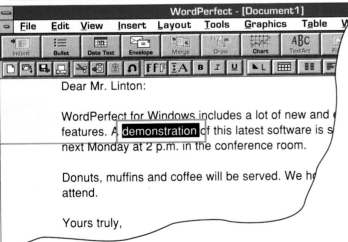

**1** Move the mouse I anywhere over the word you want to select and then quickly press the left button twice.

### TO CANCEL A TEXT SELECTION

Move the mouse I anywhere outside the selected area and then press the left button.

## Select a Sentence

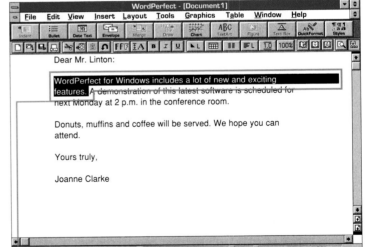

**1** Move the mouse I anywhere over the sentence you want to select and then quickly press the left button **three** times.

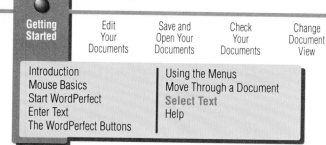

| Getting Started | Edit Your Documents | Save and Open Your Documents | Check Your Documents | Change Document View | Format Your Documents | Create a Table | Print Your Documents | Use Multiple Documents | Using Graphics | Merge Documents |

Introduction
Mouse Basics
Start WordPerfect
Enter Text
The WordPerfect Buttons

Using the Menus
Move Through a Document
**Select Text**
Help

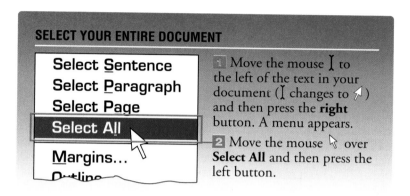

**SELECT YOUR ENTIRE DOCUMENT**

Select **S**entence
Select **P**aragraph
Select Pa**g**e
**Select All**

**M**argins...

**1** Move the mouse I to the left of the text in your document (I changes to ⬈) and then press the **right** button. A menu appears.

**2** Move the mouse ⬉ over **Select All** and then press the left button.

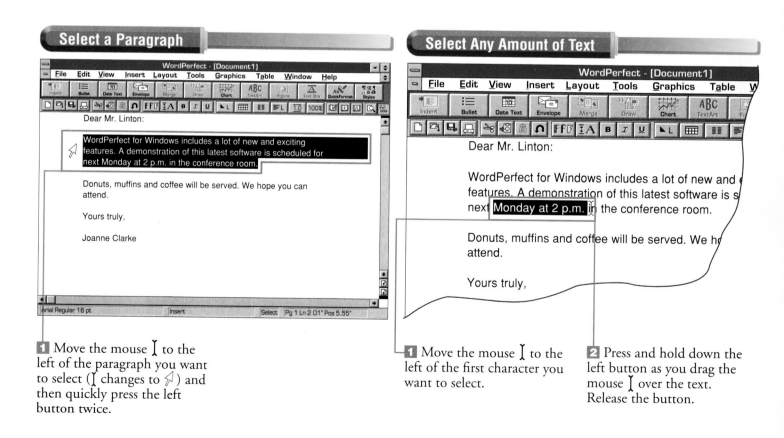

**Select a Paragraph**

Dear Mr. Linton:

WordPerfect for Windows includes a lot of new and exciting features. A demonstration of this latest software is scheduled for next Monday at 2 p.m. in the conference room.

Donuts, muffins and coffee will be served. We hope you can attend.

Yours truly,

Joanne Clarke

**1** Move the mouse I to the left of the paragraph you want to select (I changes to ⬈) and then quickly press the left button twice.

**Select Any Amount of Text**

Dear Mr. Linton:

WordPerfect for Windows includes a lot of new and features. A demonstration of this latest software is s next Monday at 2 p.m. in the conference room.

Donuts, muffins and coffee will be served. We h attend.

Yours truly,

**1** Move the mouse I to the left of the first character you want to select.

**2** Press and hold down the left button as you drag the mouse I over the text. Release the button.

# HELP

If you forget how to perform a task, you can use the WordPerfect Help feature to obtain information. This can save you time by eliminating the need to refer to other sources.

## Help

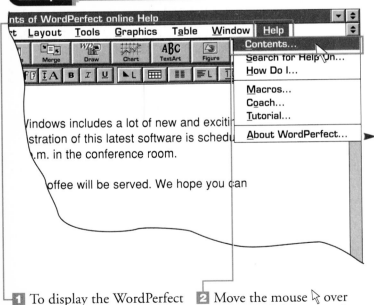

**1** To display the WordPerfect Help Contents, move the mouse ⬭ over **Help** and then press the left button.

**2** Move the mouse ⬭ over **Contents** and then press the left button.

◆ The **WordPerfect Help** window appears.

**3** Move the mouse ⬭ over an item of interest (example: **How Do I**) and ⬭ changes to ⬤. Then press the left button.

Introduction
Mouse Basics
Start WordPerfect
Enter Text
The WordPerfect Buttons

Using the Menus
Move Through a Document
Select Text
Help

## TO RECEIVE HELP ON A BUTTON

**1** Press Shift + F1 and ⊠ changes to ⊠(?).
**2** Move the mouse ⊠(?) over the button of interest (example: **Indent**) and then press the left button.

## TO RECEIVE HELP ON A MENU COMMAND

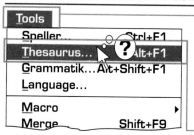

**1** To open the menu containing the command of interest, move the mouse ⊠ over the menu name (example: **Tools**) and then press the left button.

**2** Press Shift + F1 and ⊠ changes to ⊠(?).

**3** Move the mouse ⊠(?) over the command (example: **Thesaurus**) and then press the left button.

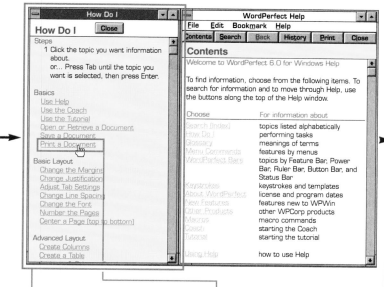

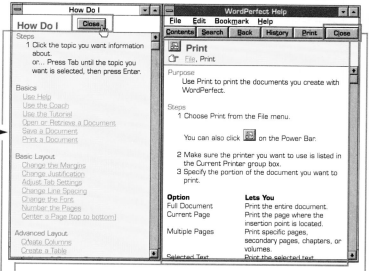

♦ The **How Do I** window appears.

**4** Move the mouse ⊠ over a topic of interest (example: **Print a Document**) and ⊠ changes to ⊠. Then press the left button.

♦ Information on the topic you selected appears.

**5** To close the **How Do I** window, move the mouse ⊠ over **Close** and then press the left button.

**6** To exit **WordPerfect Help**, move the mouse ⊠ over **Close** and then press the left button.

17

# INSERT TEXT

> WordPerfect makes it easy to edit your document. To make changes, you no longer have to retype a page or use correction fluid.

## Insert a Blank Line

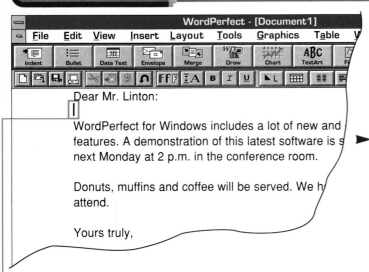

**1** Position the insertion point where you want to insert a blank line.

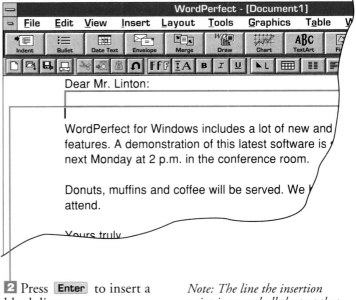

**2** Press **Enter** to insert a blank line.

*Note: The line the insertion point is on and all the text that follows move down one line.*

# IMPORTANT!

◆ Make sure you save your document to store it for future use. If you do not save your document, it will disappear when you turn off your computer.

*Note: To save a document, refer to page 34.*

## Split and Join Paragraphs

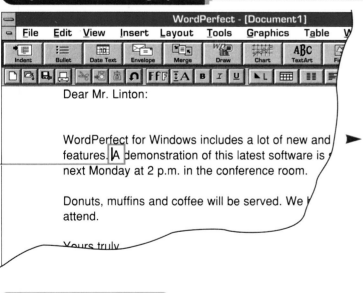

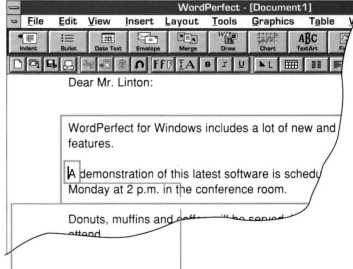

### Split a Paragraph

**1** Position the insertion point where you want to split a paragraph in two.

**2** Press **Enter** and the paragraph is split in two.

**3** To insert a blank line between the two paragraphs, press **Enter** again.

### Join Two Paragraphs

**1** Position the insertion point to the left of the first character in the second paragraph.

**2** Press **+Backspace** until the paragraphs are joined.

# INSERT TEXT

In the Insert mode, the text you type appears at the current insertion point location. The existing text moves forward to make room for the new text.

This sentence moves forward as you type.

------------------------This sentence moves forward as you type.

## Insert Text

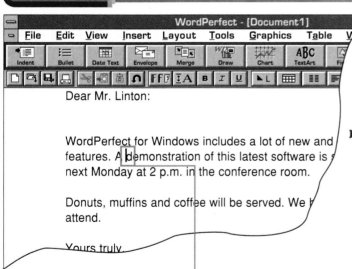

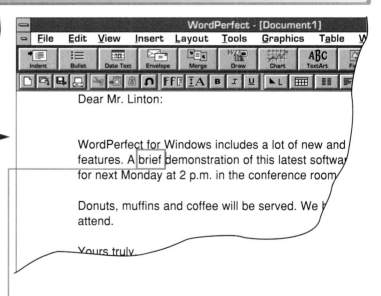

**When you start WordPerfect, the program is in the Insert mode.**

**1** Position the insertion point where you want to insert the new text.

*Note: If **Typeover** is displayed at the bottom of your screen, press* Insert *. This turns off the **Typeover** mode.*

**2** Type the text you want to insert (example: **brief**).

**3** To insert a blank space, press the **Spacebar**.

*Note: The words to the right of the inserted text are pushed forward.*

20

| Getting Started | **Edit Your Documents** | Save and Open Your Documents | Check Your Documents | Change Document View | Format Your Documents | Create a Table | Print Your Documents | Use Multiple Documents | Using Graphics | Merge Documents |

**Insert Text**
Delete Text
Undo

Undelete Text
Move Text
Copy Text

In the Typeover mode, the text you type appears at the current insertion point location. The new text replaces (types over) any existing text.

|This sentence disappears as you type.

xxxxxxxxxxxxxxxxxxxx|pears as you type.

## Typeover Text

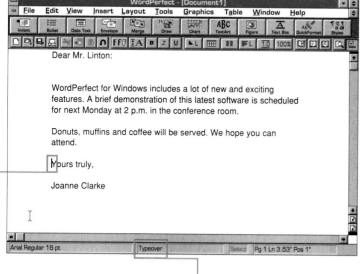

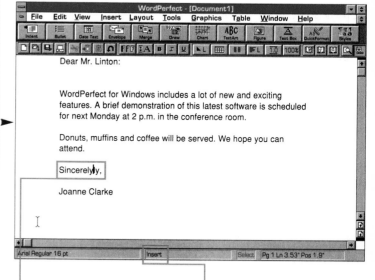

**You can use** `Insert` **to switch between the Insert and Typeover modes.**

**1** Position the insertion point to the left of the first character you want to replace.

**2** Press `Insert` to turn on the **Typeover** mode. The word **Typeover** appears at the bottom of your screen.

**3** Type the text you want to replace the existing text with (example: **Sincerely**).

*Note: To delete the extra "**ly**" at the end of **Sincerelyly**, refer to the next page.*

**4** Press `Insert` to turn off the **Typeover** mode. The word **Insert** appears at the bottom of your screen.

# DELETE TEXT

You can use Delete to remove the character to the right of the insertion point. The remaining text moves to the left.

**Delete** **Delete Characters**

WordPerfect for
features. A brief demonstration of this latest
for next Monday at 2 p.m. in the conference ro

Donuts, muffins and coffee will be served. We ho
attend.

Sincerelyly,

Joanne Clarke

Arial Regular 16 pt    Insert    Select

➤

WordPerfect for
features. A brief demonstration of this latest
for next Monday at 2 p.m. in the conference ro

Donuts, muffins and coffee will be served. We h
attend.

Sincerely,

Joanne Clarke

Arial Regular 16 pt    Insert    Select

**1** Position the insertion point to the left of the character you want to delete (example: the second **l** in Sincerelyly).

**2** Press Delete once for each character you want to delete (example: press Delete twice).

You can also delete characters using this key. Position the insertion point to the right of the character(s) you want to delete and then press ◆Backspace .

←Backspace

Insert Text    Undelete Text
**Delete Text**    Move Text
Undo    Copy Text

You can use **Delete** to remove the blank line the insertion point is on. The remaining text moves up one line.

## Delete    Delete a Blank Line

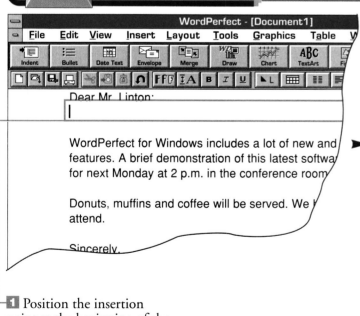

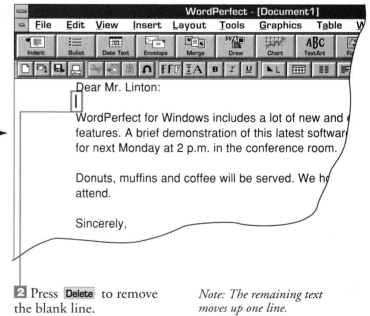

**1** Position the insertion point at the beginning of the blank line you want to delete.

**2** Press **Delete** to remove the blank line.

*Note: The remaining text moves up one line.*

23

> You can use Delete to remove text you have selected. The remaining text moves up or to the left.

## Delete — Delete Selected Text

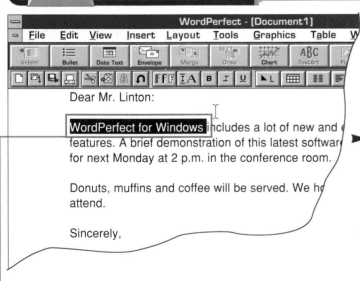

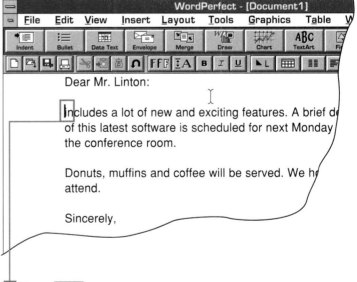

**1** Select the text you want to delete.

*Note: To select text, refer to page 14.*

**2** Press Delete to remove the text.

24

WordPerfect remembers the last change you made to your document. If you regret this change, you can cancel it by using the Undo feature.

Undo

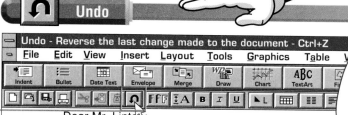

Undo - Reverse the last change made to the document - Ctrl+Z

Dear Mr. Linton:

Includes a lot of new and exciting features. A brief d[...] of this latest software is scheduled for next Monday [...] the conference room.

Donuts, muffins and coffee will be served. We h[...] attend.

Sincerely,

WordPerfect - [Document1]

Dear Mr. Linton:

WordPerfect for Windows includes a lot of new and [...] features. A brief demonstration of this latest softwar[...] for next Monday at 2 p.m. in the conference room.

Donuts, muffins and coffee will be served. We h[...] attend.

Sincerely,

**1** Move the mouse ⏳ over ↺ and then press the left button.

**SHORT CUT**

Press Ctrl + Z

◆ WordPerfect reverses the last change you made to your document.

*Note: The last change you made to your document may include any editing or formatting change.*

# UNDELETE TEXT

*If you accidentally delete text, it is not permanently lost. WordPerfect remembers your last three text deletions and can restore them.*

## Undelete Text

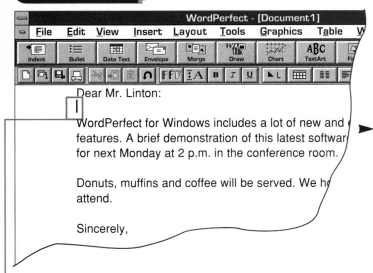

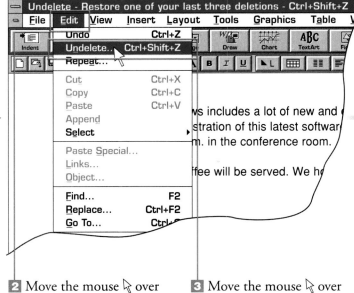

**1** Position the insertion point where you want the deleted text to reappear.

**2** Move the mouse ♀ over **Edit** and then press the left button.

**3** Move the mouse ♀ over **Undelete** and then press the left button.

◆ The **Undelete** dialog box appears.

Getting Started | Edit Your Documents | Save and Open Your Documents | Check Your Documents | Change Document View | Format Your Documents | Create a Table | Print Your Documents | Use Multiple Documents | Using Graphics | Merge Documents

Insert Text | Undelete Text
Delete Text | Move Text
Undo | Copy Text

**It is important to understand the differences between the Undo and Undelete feature.**

*Note: To use the* **Undo** *feature, refer to page 25.*

## UNDO

◆ Undo can restore your **last** text deletion.

◆ Undo only restores deleted text if you use the command before making another change to your document.

◆ Undo places the deleted text where it was originally located in your document.

## UNDELETE

◆ Undelete can restore your **last three** text deletions.

◆ Undelete can restore deleted text at any time.

◆ You must indicate where you want the deleted text placed in your document.

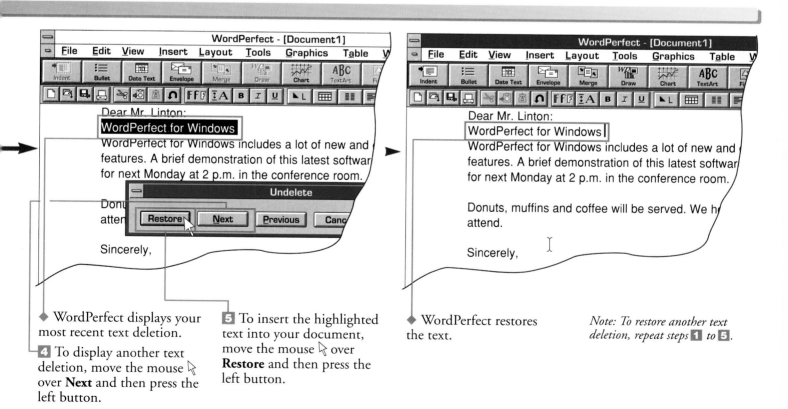

◆ WordPerfect displays your most recent text deletion.

**4** To display another text deletion, move the mouse ⌖ over **Next** and then press the left button.

*Note: To cycle through your last three text deletions, repeat step 4.*

**5** To insert the highlighted text into your document, move the mouse ⌖ over **Restore** and then press the left button.

◆ WordPerfect restores the text.

*Note: To restore another text deletion, repeat steps 1 to 5.*

# MOVE TEXT

You can move text from one location in your document to another. WordPerfect "cuts" the text and "pastes" it in a new location. The original text disappears.

## Move Text

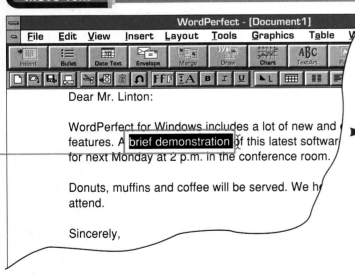

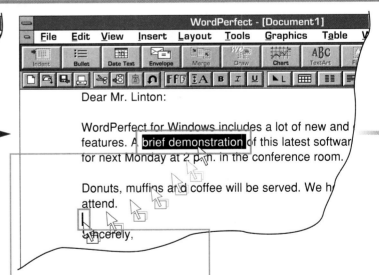

**1** Select the text you want to move.

*Note: To select text, refer to page 14.*

**2** Move the mouse I anywhere over the selected text and I becomes ↖.

**3** Press and hold down the left button as you drag the mouse ↖ where you want to move the text.

*Note: The text will appear where the insertion point flashes on your screen.*

Getting
Started

**Edit
Your
Documents**

Save and
Open Your
Documents

Check
Your
Documents

Change
Document
View

Format
Your
Documents

Create
a Table

Print
Your
Documents

Use
Multiple
Documents

Using
Graphics

Merge
Documents

Insert Text    Undelete Text
Delete Text    **Move Text**
Undo         Copy Text

**You can reverse the
last change you made
to your document.**

◆ To move the text back to its
original location, move the
mouse ⊾ over ⟲ and then
press the left button.

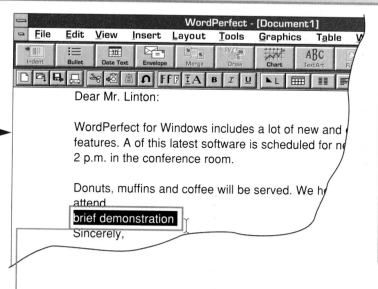

**4** Release the left button
and the text moves to the
new location.

**You can also move text
using these buttons.**

**1** Select the text you want to move.

**2** Move the mouse ⊾ over ✂ and
then press the left button. The
selected text disappears from your
screen.

**3** Position the insertion point where
you want to move the text.

**4** Move the mouse ⊾ over 📋 and
then press the left button. The text
moves to the new location.

# COPY TEXT

You can copy text from one location in your document to another. WordPerfect "copies" the text and "pastes" the copy in a new location. The original text remains in its place.

## Copy Text

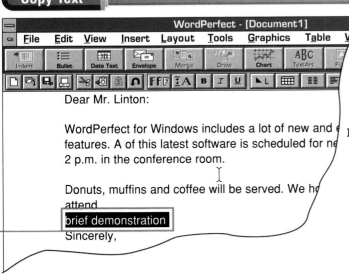

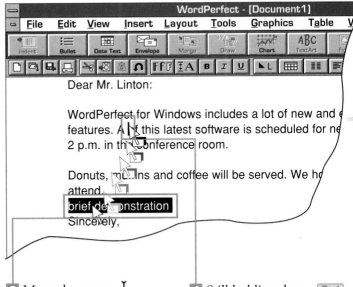

**1** Select the text you want to copy.

*Note: To select text, refer to page 14.*

**2** Move the mouse I anywhere over the selected text and I becomes ↖.

**3** Press and hold down Ctrl.

**4** Still holding down Ctrl, press and hold down the left button as you drag the mouse ↖ where you want to place the copy.

*Note: The text will appear where the insertion point flashes on your screen.*

| Getting Started | Edit Your Documents | Save and Open Your Documents | Check Your Documents | Change Document View | Format Your Documents | Create a Table | Print Your Documents | Use Multiple Documents | Using Graphics | Merge Documents |

Insert Text    Undelete Text
Delete Text    Move Text
Undo        **Copy Text**

**Tip**

**You can reverse the last change you made to your document.**

◆ To remove the copy, move the mouse ⟍ over 🔄 and then press the left button.

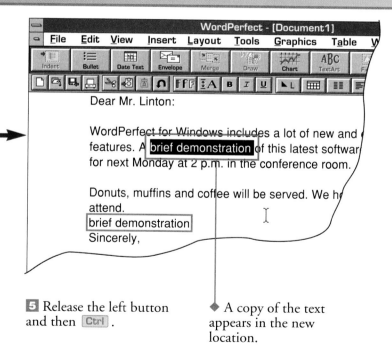

Dear Mr. Linton:

WordPerfect for Windows includes a lot of new and features. A brief demonstration of this latest software for next Monday at 2 p.m. in the conference room.

Donuts, muffins and coffee will be served. We h attend.

brief demonstration
Sincerely,

**5** Release the left button and then Ctrl.

◆ A copy of the text appears in the new location.

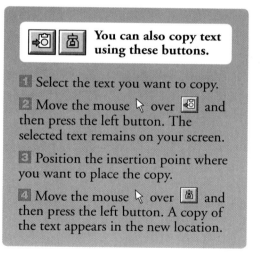

**You can also copy text using these buttons.**

**1** Select the text you want to copy.

**2** Move the mouse ⟍ over 🔳 and then press the left button. The selected text remains on your screen.

**3** Position the insertion point where you want to place the copy.

**4** Move the mouse ⟍ over 🔳 and then press the left button. A copy of the text appears in the new location.

31

**Hard Drive (C:)**

The hard drive stores your programs and data. It contains many directories to help organize your information.

**Directories**

A directory usually contains related information. For example, WordPerfect stores your document files in the **wpdocs** directory.

Your computer stores programs and data in devices called drives. A drive contains directories to help organize your information. Think of a drive as a filing cabinet and directories as drawers and folders.

**Files**

When you save a document, WordPerfect stores it as a file.

**Most computers have one hard drive and one or two floppy drives to store information.**

### Hard drive (C:)

◆ The hard drive magnetically stores information inside your computer. It is called drive **C**.

*Note: Your computer may be set up to have additional hard drives (example: drive **D**).*

### Floppy drives (A: and B:)

◆ A floppy drive stores information on removable diskettes (or floppy disks). A diskette operates slower and stores less data than a hard drive.

Diskettes are used to:
• Load new programs.
• Store backup copies of data.
• Transfer data to other computers.

If your computer has only one floppy drive, it is called drive **A**.

If your computer has two floppy drives, the second drive is called drive **B**.

# SAVE A NEW DOCUMENT

You should save your document to store it for future use. This enables you to later retrieve the document for reviewing or editing.

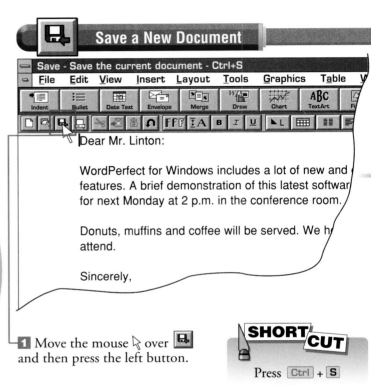

**1** Move the mouse ↖ over 🖫 and then press the left button.

**SHORT CUT**

Press Ctrl + S

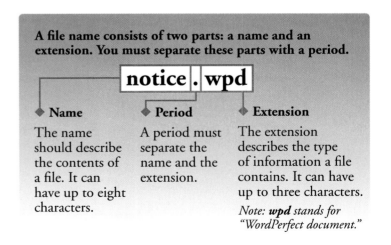

A file name consists of two parts: a name and an extension. You must separate these parts with a period.

**notice . wpd**

◆ **Name**

The name should describe the contents of a file. It can have up to eight characters.

◆ **Period**

A period must separate the name and the extension.

◆ **Extension**

The extension describes the type of information a file contains. It can have up to three characters.

*Note: **wpd** stands for "WordPerfect document."*

| Getting Started | Edit Your Documents | **Save and Open Your Documents** | Check Your Documents | Change Document View | Format Your Documents | Create a Table | Print Your Documents | Use Multiple Documents | Using Graphics | Merge Documents |

Introduction
**Save a New Document**
Save a Document to a Diskette
Exit WordPerfect
Open a Document

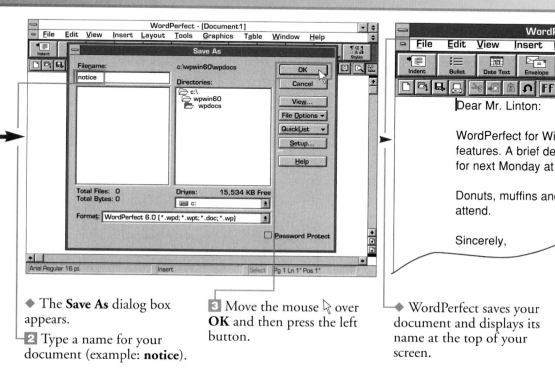

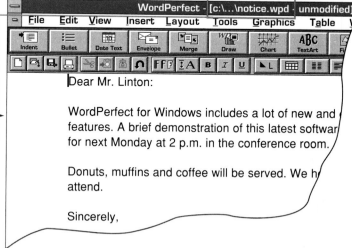

◆ The **Save As** dialog box appears.

**2** Type a name for your document (example: **notice**).

**3** Move the mouse ⬚ over **OK** and then press the left button.

◆ WordPerfect saves your document and displays its name at the top of your screen.

◆ WordPerfect automatically adds the extension **wpd** to the file name (example: **notice.wpd**).

## Rules for Naming a File

**A file name *can* contain the following characters:**

◆ The letters A to Z, upper or lower case

◆ The numbers 0 to 9

◆ The symbols
_ ^ $ ~ ! # % & { } @ ( )

**A file name *cannot* contain the following characters:**

◆ A comma (,)

◆ A blank space

◆ The symbols
+ = \ / ? < > *

**Each file in a directory must have a unique name.**

letter.wpd
note1q.wpd
test.wpd
training.wpd

# SAVE A DOCUMENT TO A DISKETTE

As a precaution, you should save your document to a diskette. You can then use this copy to replace any lost data if your hard drive fails or you accidentally erase the file.

## Save a Document to a Diskette

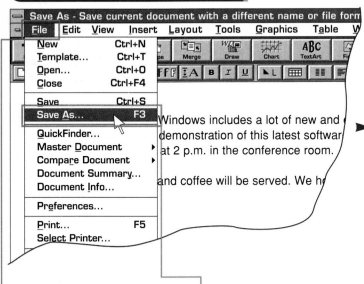

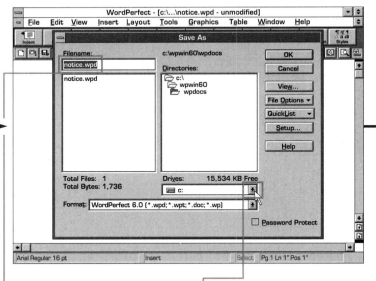

**1** Insert a diskette into a floppy drive (example: **a:**).

**2** Move the mouse ⇧ over **File** and then press the left button.

**3** Move the mouse ⇧ over **Save As** and then press the left button.

◆ The **Save As** dialog box appears.

◆ The **Filename:** box displays the current file name (example: **notice.wpd**).

*Note: To save your document with a different name, type a new name.*

**4** To change the current drive (c:) to a floppy drive (a: or b:), move the mouse ⇧ over the arrow in the **Drives:** box and then press the left button.

◆ After you save your document, you may want to make additional changes. You can use the **Save As** command to save your revised document with a new name. This way, you still have a copy of the old version in case you regret any changes you made.

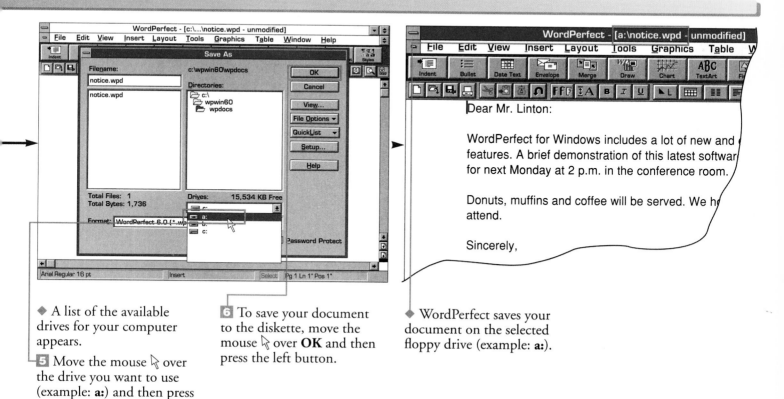

◆ A list of the available drives for your computer appears.

**5** Move the mouse ♦ over the drive you want to use (example: **a:**) and then press the left button.

**6** To save your document to the diskette, move the mouse ♦ over **OK** and then press the left button.

◆ WordPerfect saves your document on the selected floppy drive (example: **a:**).

37

# EXIT WORDPERFECT

You can exit WordPerfect to return to the Windows Program Manager.

## Exit WordPerfect

### IMPORTANT!

You must always exit WordPerfect and Windows before turning your computer off. Failure to do so may result in damage or loss of valuable information.

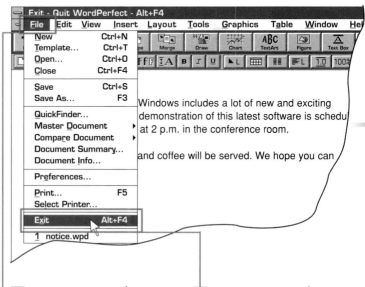

**1** Move the mouse ⟋ over **File** and then press the left button.

**2** Move the mouse ⟋ over **Exit** and then press the left button.

Introduction
Save a New Document
Save a Document to a Diskette
**Exit WordPerfect**
Open a Document

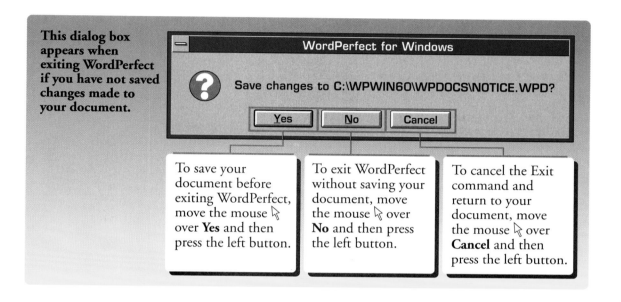

**This dialog box appears when exiting WordPerfect if you have not saved changes made to your document.**

To save your document before exiting WordPerfect, move the mouse ⬐ over **Yes** and then press the left button.

To exit WordPerfect without saving your document, move the mouse ⬐ over **No** and then press the left button.

To cancel the Exit command and return to your document, move the mouse ⬐ over **Cancel** and then press the left button.

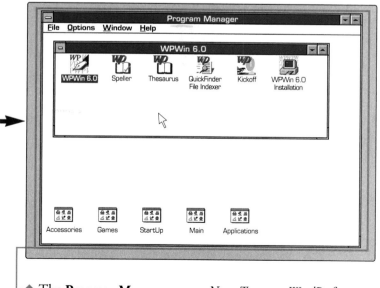

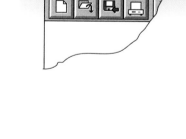

**SHORTCUT**

◆ To exit WordPerfect, move the mouse ⬐ over the **Control-menu box** and then quickly press the left button twice.

◆ The **Program Manager** window appears.

*Note: To restart WordPerfect, refer to page 6.*

39

# OPEN A DOCUMENT

You can open a saved document and display it on your screen. This enables you to view and make changes to your document.

## Open a Document

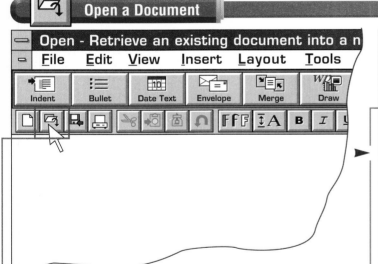

**1** Move the mouse ⇖ over 🗁 and then press the left button.

◆ The **Open File** dialog box appears.

**2** Move the mouse ⇖ over the name of the file you want to open (example: **notice.wpd**) and then press the left button.

**3** To preview the file before opening it, move the mouse ⇖ over **View** and then press the left button.

Introduction
Save a New Document
Save a Document to a Diskette
Exit WordPerfect
**Open a Document**

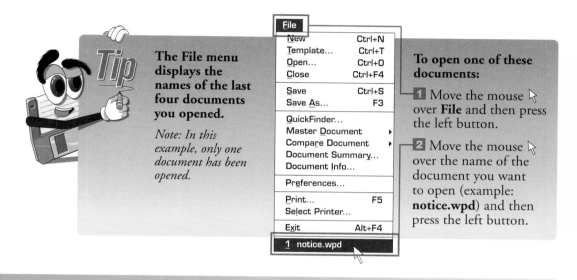

The File menu
displays the
names of the last
four documents
you opened.

*Note: In this
example, only one
document has been
opened.*

**To open one of these
documents:**

**1** Move the mouse 🖑
over **File** and then press
the left button.

**2** Move the mouse 🖑
over the name of the
document you want
to open (example:
**notice.wpd**) and then
press the left button.

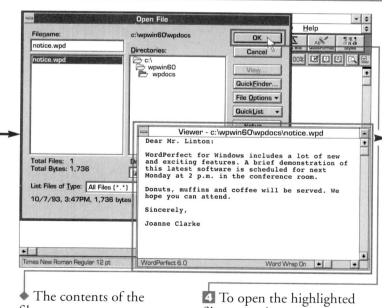

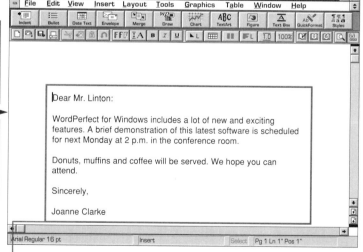

◆ The contents of the
file appear.

*Note: To view the contents
of another file, repeat step **2**.*

**4** To open the highlighted
file, move the mouse 🖑 over
**OK** and then press the left
button.

◆ WordPerfect opens the
document and displays it on
your screen. You can now
make changes to the
document.

◆ To work faster in
WordPerfect, display the
document in the Draft
mode.

*Note: To change modes,
refer to page 54.*

# FIND
# TEXT

You can use the Find feature to locate a word or phrase in your document.

## Find Text

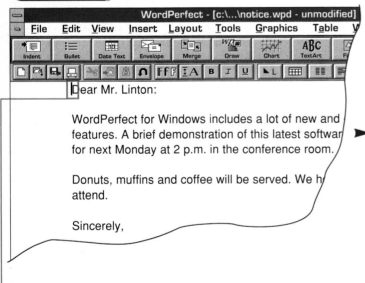

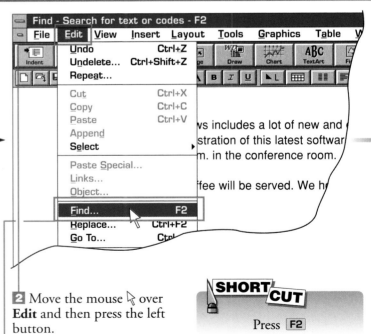

**1** Position the insertion point where you want the search to begin.

**2** Move the mouse ⌖ over **Edit** and then press the left button.

**3** Move the mouse ⌖ over **Find** and then press the left button.

**SHORT CUT**

Press **F2**

42

# FIND AND REPLACE TEXT

You can use the Replace feature to locate and replace every occurrence of a word or phrase in your document. This is ideal if you have frequently misspelled a word.

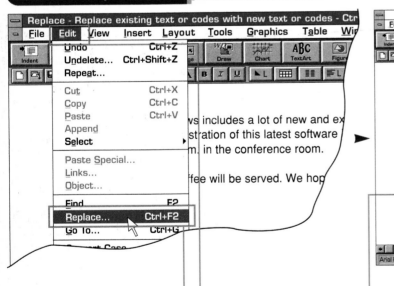

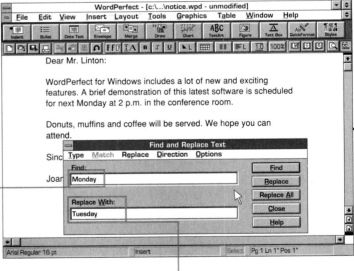

◆ The **Find and Replace Text** dialog box appears.

**1** Position the insertion point where you want the Replace feature to begin.

**2** Move the mouse ⅍ over **Edit** and then press the left button.

**3** Move the mouse ⅍ over **Replace** and then press the left button.

**4** Type the text you want to find (example: **Monday**).

**5** Press [Tab] to move to the **Replace With:** box.

**6** Type the text you want to replace the searched word with (example: **Tuesday**).

Getting
Started

Edit
Your
Documents

Save and
Open Your
Documents

**Check
Your
Documents**

Change
Document
View

Format
Your
Documents

Create
a Table

Print
Your
Documents

Use
Multiple
Documents

Using
Graphics

Merge
Documents

Find Text
**Find and Replace Text**
Speller
Thesaurus
Grammatik

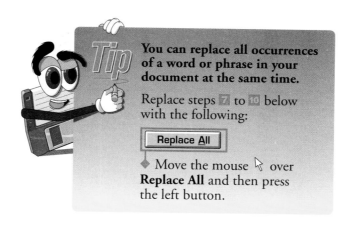

**You can replace all occurrences of a word or phrase in your document at the same time.**

Replace steps **7** to **10** below with the following:

> **Replace All**

◆ Move the mouse ⌖ over **Replace All** and then press the left button.

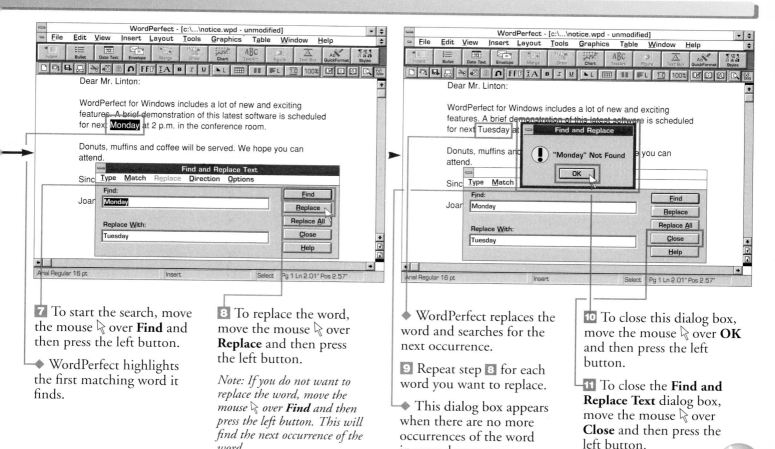

**7** To start the search, move the mouse ⌖ over **Find** and then press the left button.

◆ WordPerfect highlights the first matching word it finds.

**8** To replace the word, move the mouse ⌖ over **Replace** and then press the left button.

*Note: If you do not want to replace the word, move the mouse ⌖ over **Find** and then press the left button. This will find the next occurrence of the word.*

◆ WordPerfect replaces the word and searches for the next occurrence.

**9** Repeat step **8** for each word you want to replace.

◆ This dialog box appears when there are no more occurrences of the word in your document.

**10** To close this dialog box, move the mouse ⌖ over **OK** and then press the left button.

**11** To close the **Find and Replace Text** dialog box, move the mouse ⌖ over **Close** and then press the left button.

The Speller enables you to find and correct spelling errors in your document.

WordPerfect compares every word in your document to words in its dictionary. If a word does not exist in the dictionary, WordPerfect considers it misspelled.

WP Dictionary

xpanded 6.0 Version

Theery
Theory

## Spell Check Your Document

| The Speller finds: | Example: |
|---|---|
| ◆ Misspelled words | The girl is six **yeers** old. |
| ◆ Duplicate words | The girl is **six six** years old. |
| ◆ Capitalization errors | **TH**e girl is six years old. |

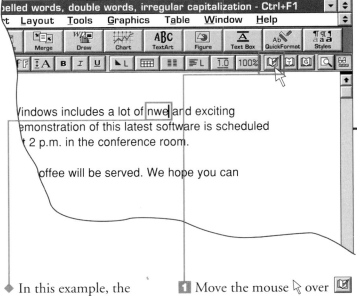

◆ In this example, the spelling of **new** was changed to **nwe**.

**1** Move the mouse ⟍ over ▥ and then press the left button.

*Note: To spell check a section of your document, select the text before performing step* **1**. *To select text, refer to page 14.*

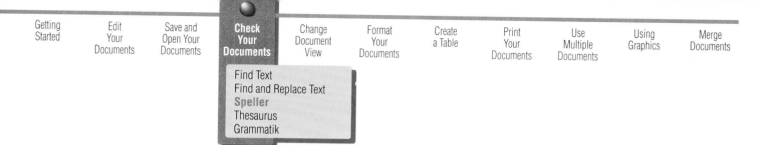

Getting Started    Edit Your Documents    Save and Open Your Documents    **Check Your Documents**    Change Document View    Format Your Documents    Create a Table    Print Your Documents    Use Multiple Documents    Using Graphics    Merge Documents

Find Text
Find and Replace Text
Speller
Thesaurus
Grammatik

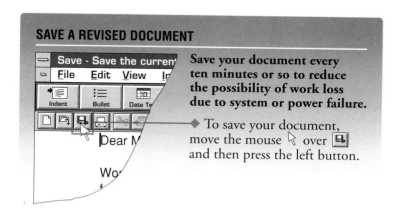

**SAVE A REVISED DOCUMENT**

Save your document every ten minutes or so to reduce the possibility of work loss due to system or power failure.

◆ To save your document, move the mouse � over ▣ and then press the left button.

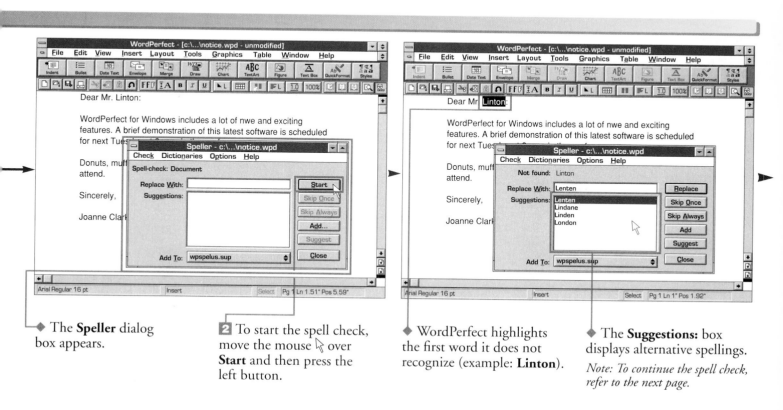

◆ The **Speller** dialog box appears.

**2** To start the spell check, move the mouse � over **Start** and then press the left button.

◆ WordPerfect highlights the first word it does not recognize (example: **Linton**).

◆ The **Suggestions:** box displays alternative spellings.

*Note: To continue the spell check, refer to the next page.*

47

## Spell Check Your Document (continued)

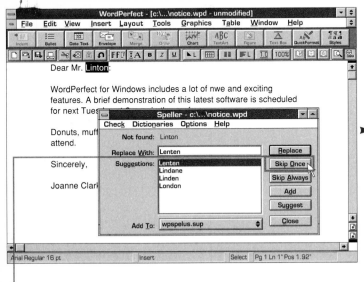

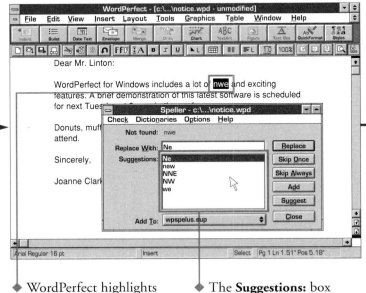

**3** If you do not want to change the spelling of the highlighted word in your document, move the mouse ⬚ over **Skip Once** and then press the left button.

*Note: To change the spelling of the word, perform steps* **4** *and* **5**.

◆ WordPerfect highlights the next word it does not recognize (example: **nwe**).

◆ The **Suggestions:** box displays alternative spellings.

## SPELLER OPTIONS

**Replace**

Replaces the misspelled word in your document with the text in the **Replace With:** box.

**Skip Always**

Keeps the current spelling of the word and skips every occurrence in the document.

**Skip Once**

Keeps the current spelling of the word in this instance only.

**Add**

Adds the word to the WordPerfect dictionary. The Speller then considers the word correctly spelled in all future documents.

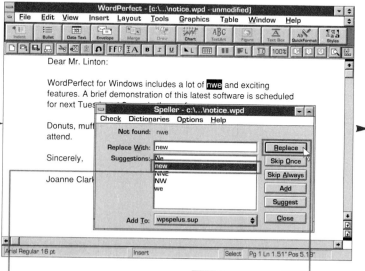

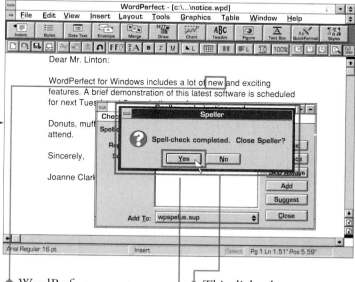

**4** To select the correct spelling, move the mouse ⍾ over the word you want to use (example: **new**) and then press the left button.

**5** To replace the misspelled word in your document with the correct spelling, move the mouse ⍾ over **Replace** and then press the left button.

◆ WordPerfect corrects the word and continues checking your document.

**6** Repeat step **3** (or steps **4** and **5**) until WordPerfect finishes checking your document.

◆ This dialog box appears when the spell check is complete.

**7** To close the Speller, move the mouse ⍾ over **Yes** and then press the left button.

To cancel the Speller at any time, move the mouse ⍾ over `Close` and then press the left button.

# THESAURUS

To add variety to your writing, you can use the WordPerfect Thesaurus. This feature enables you to replace a word in your document with one that is more suitable.

## Using the Thesaurus

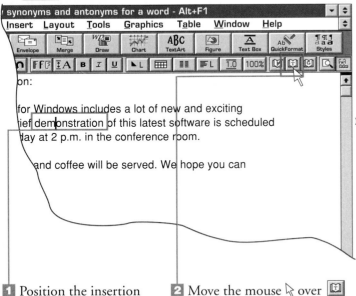

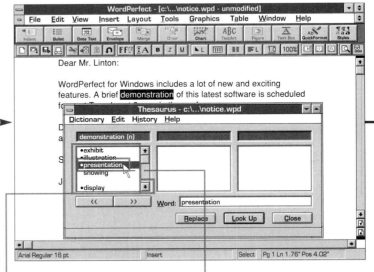

**1** Position the insertion point anywhere in the word you want to look up (example: **demonstration**).

**2** Move the mouse ⌐ over 📖 and then press the left button.

◆ The **Thesaurus** dialog box appears.

◆ This area displays a list of alternative words.

**3** To view additional choices, move the mouse ⌐ over the down arrow ▼ and then press the left button.

**4** To display words related to an item in the list, move the mouse ⌐ over the word and then quickly press the left button twice.

*Note: This only works for words displaying the (●) symbol.*

Find Text
Find and Replace Text
Speller
**Thesaurus**
Grammatik

## LOOK UP ANOTHER WORD

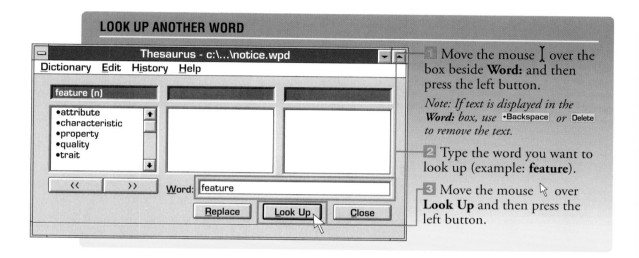

**1** Move the mouse I over the box beside **Word:** and then press the left button.

*Note: If text is displayed in the **Word:** box, use* +Backspace *or* Delete *to remove the text.*

**2** Type the word you want to look up (example: **feature**).

**3** Move the mouse ⬚ over **Look Up** and then press the left button.

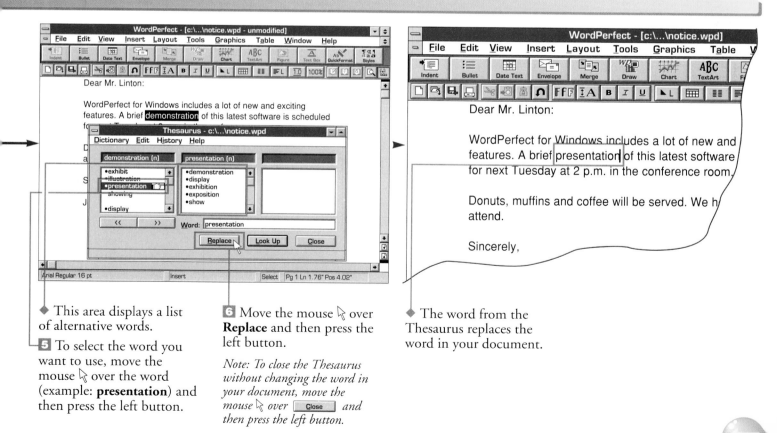

◆ This area displays a list of alternative words.

**5** To select the word you want to use, move the mouse ⬚ over the word (example: **presentation**) and then press the left button.

**6** Move the mouse ⬚ over **Replace** and then press the left button.

*Note: To close the Thesaurus without changing the word in your document, move the mouse ⬚ over* Close *and then press the left button.*

◆ The word from the Thesaurus replaces the word in your document.

# GRAMMATIK

You can use Grammatik to check for spelling, grammar and punctuation errors. This will improve the accuracy of your document.

## Check for Grammar and Spelling Errors

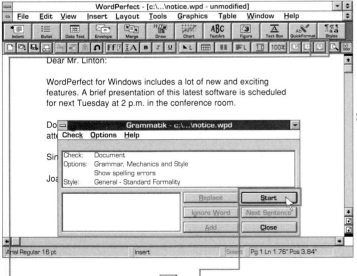

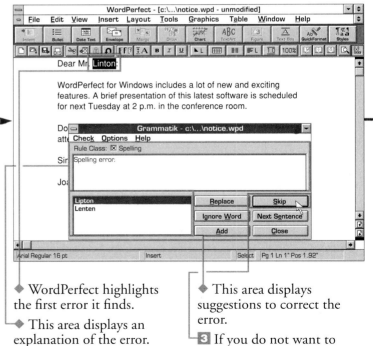

**1** Move the mouse ⌖ over ⊞ and then press the left button.

◆ The **Grammatik** dialog box appears.

**2** To start the grammar check, move the mouse ⌖ over **Start** and then press the left button.

◆ WordPerfect highlights the first error it finds.

◆ This area displays an explanation of the error.

◆ This area displays suggestions to correct the error.

**3** If you do not want to correct the error, move the mouse ⌖ over **Skip** and then press the left button.

Find Text
Find and Replace Text
Speller
Thesaurus
Grammatik

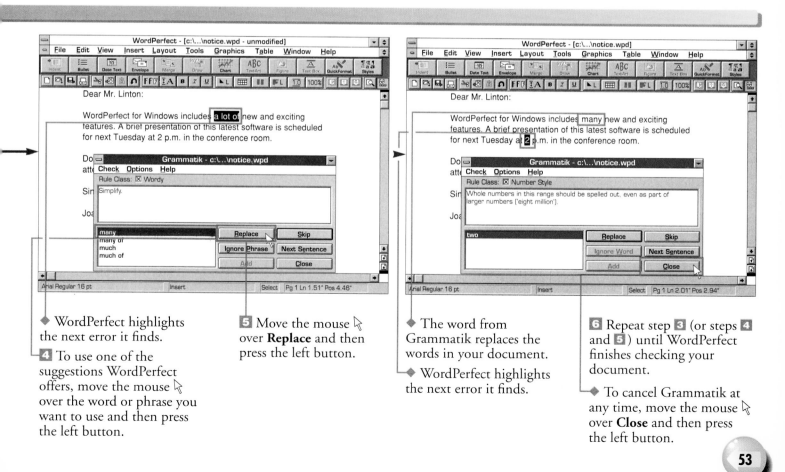

This dialog box appears when WordPerfect completes the grammar check.

◆ To close Grammatik, move the mouse over **Yes** and then press the left button.

◆ WordPerfect highlights the next error it finds.

**4** To use one of the suggestions WordPerfect offers, move the mouse over the word or phrase you want to use and then press the left button.

**5** Move the mouse over **Replace** and then press the left button.

◆ The word from Grammatik replaces the words in your document.

◆ WordPerfect highlights the next error it finds.

**6** Repeat step **3** (or steps **4** and **5**) until WordPerfect finishes checking your document.

◆ To cancel Grammatik at any time, move the mouse over **Close** and then press the left button.

53

WordPerfect offers three different modes you can use to display your document. You can choose the mode that best suits your needs.

## Change the Document Mode

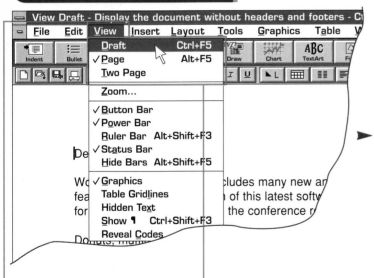

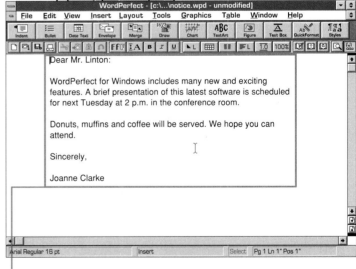

**1** Move the mouse ⟍ over **View** and then press the left button.

**2** Move the mouse ⟍ over the mode you want to use (example: **Draft**) and then press the left button.

◆ Your document appears in the new mode.

## The WordPerfect Modes

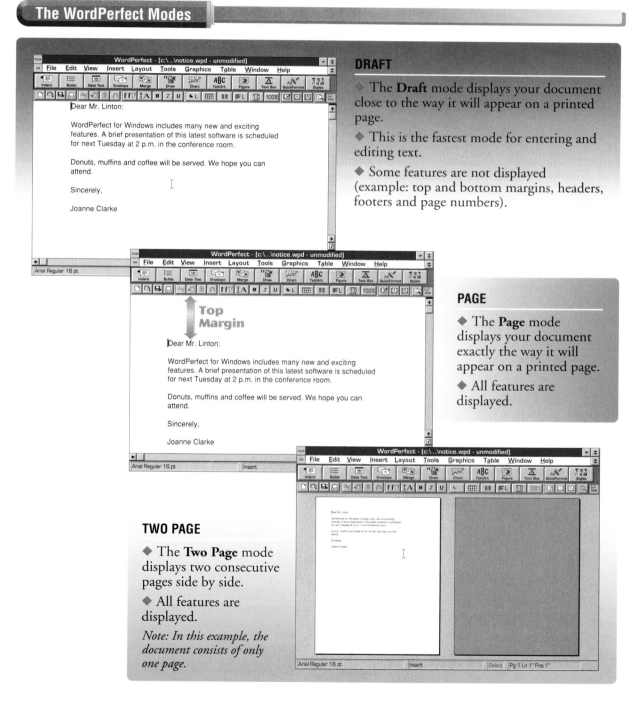

### DRAFT

◆ The **Draft** mode displays your document close to the way it will appear on a printed page.

◆ This is the fastest mode for entering and editing text.

◆ Some features are not displayed (example: top and bottom margins, headers, footers and page numbers).

### PAGE

◆ The **Page** mode displays your document exactly the way it will appear on a printed page.

◆ All features are displayed.

### TWO PAGE

◆ The **Two Page** mode displays two consecutive pages side by side.

◆ All features are displayed.

*Note: In this example, the document consists of only one page.*

# ZOOM DOCUMENT

WordPerfect enables you to enlarge or reduce the display of text on your screen. You can magnify the document to help read small text or shrink the document to view all the text on a page.

## Zoom Document

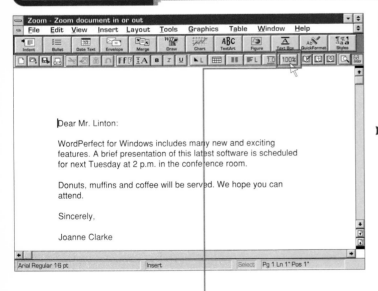

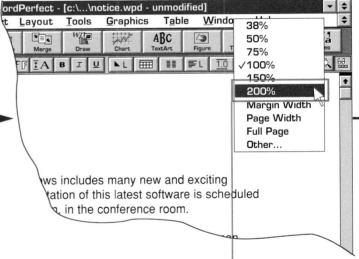

**In this example, the document is displayed in the Page mode.**

*Note: To change modes, refer to page 54.*

**1** Move the mouse ⌖ over `100%` and then press and hold down the left button.

**2** Still holding down the button, move the mouse ⌖ over the zoom percentage you want to use (example: **200%**).

Change Modes
**Zoom Document**
Select a Button Bar

## IMPORTANT!

You cannot use the Zoom feature if your document is displayed in the Two Page mode.

*Note: For more information on the Two Page mode, refer to page 55.*

**DISPLAY FULL PAGE**

To quickly display an entire page, move the mouse ▷ over 🔍 and then press the left button.

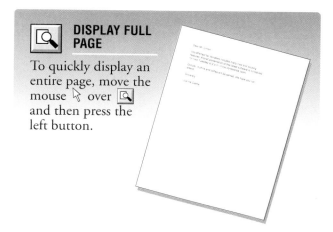

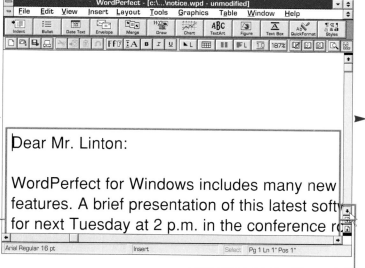

Dear Mr. Linton:

WordPerfect for Windows includes many new features. A brief presentation of this latest soft for next Tuesday at 2 p.m. in the conference r

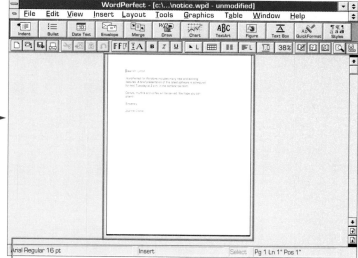

**3** Release the button and the document appears in the new zoom percentage.

◆ You can edit your document as usual.

**4** To scroll through your document, move the mouse ▷ over the down arrow ▼ and then press the left button.

◆ To display your document in another zoom percentage (example: **Full Page**), repeat steps **1** to **3**.

A Button Bar enables you to quickly select commonly used commands. You can display one of twelve Button Bars offered by WordPerfect.

## Select a Button Bar

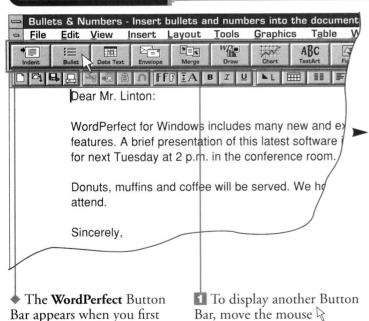

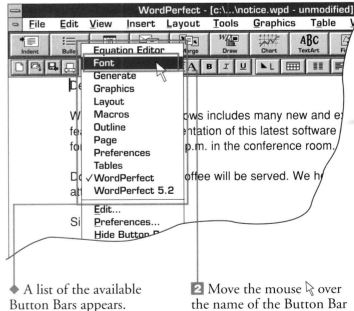

◆ The **WordPerfect** Button Bar appears when you first start WordPerfect.

**1** To display another Button Bar, move the mouse �R anywhere over the bar and then press the **right** mouse button.

◆ A list of the available Button Bars appears.

**2** Move the mouse �R over the name of the Button Bar you want to display (example: **Font**) and then press the left button.

| Getting Started | Edit Your Documents | Save and Open Your Documents | Check Your Documents | **Change Document View** | Format Your Documents | Create a Table | Print Your Documents | Use Multiple Documents | Using Graphics | Merge Documents |

Change Modes
Zoom Document
**Select a Button Bar**

**Each Button Bar contains related buttons that enable you to quickly perform a task. Here are some examples:**

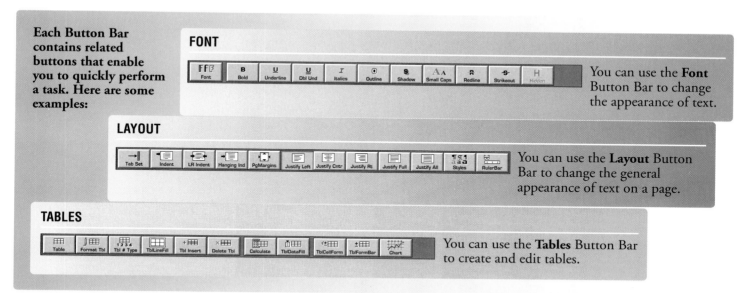

FONT

You can use the **Font** Button Bar to change the appearance of text.

LAYOUT

You can use the **Layout** Button Bar to change the general appearance of text on a page.

TABLES

You can use the **Tables** Button Bar to create and edit tables.

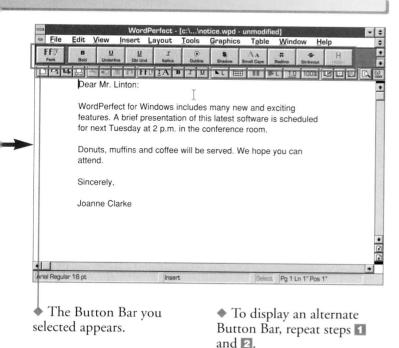

◆ The Button Bar you selected appears.

◆ To display an alternate Button Bar, repeat steps **1** and **2**.

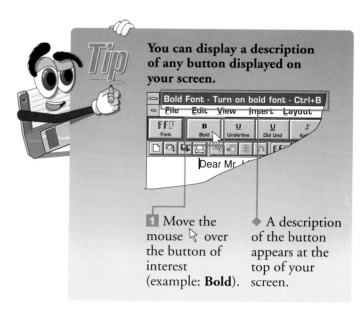

**You can display a description of any button displayed on your screen.**

**1** Move the mouse ⓚ over the button of interest (example: **Bold**).

◆ A description of the button appears at the top of your screen.

You can enhance the appearance of your document by aligning text in different ways. WordPerfect offers several alignment options.

Right
Center
Left
Full

## Justify Text

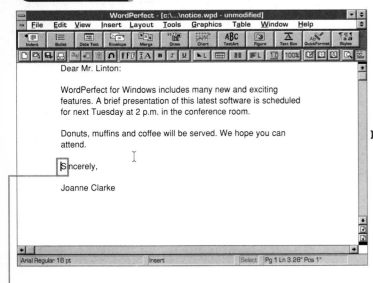

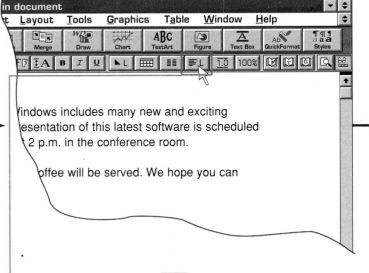

**1** Position the insertion point where you want the new justification to begin.

*Note: To change the justification of a section of text, select the text you want to change. To select text, refer to page 14.*

**2** Move the mouse ⟍ over ▤L and then press and hold down the left button.

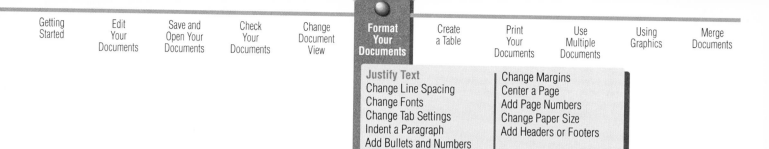

**Justify Text**
Change Line Spacing
Change Fonts
Change Tab Settings
Indent a Paragraph
Add Bullets and Numbers

Change Margins
Center a Page
Add Page Numbers
Change Paper Size
Add Headers or Footers

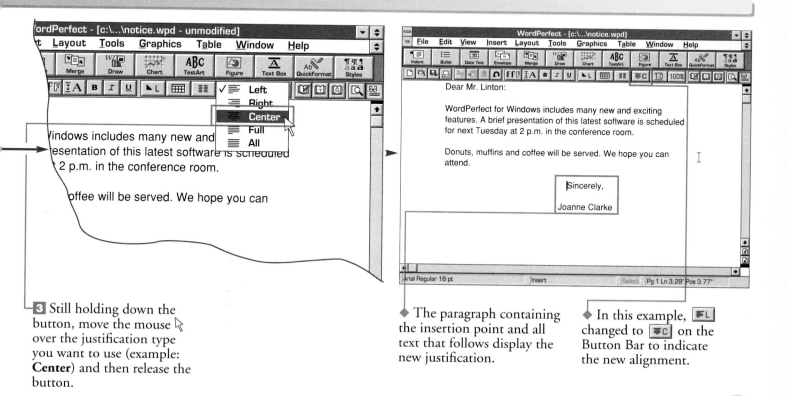

**3** Still holding down the button, move the mouse over the justification type you want to use (example: **Center**) and then release the button.

◆ The paragraph containing the insertion point and all text that follows display the new justification.

◆ In this example, ▣L changed to ▣C on the Button Bar to indicate the new alignment.

61

◆ Single spacing (1.0)
*This is the initial (or default) setting.*

◆ Double spacing (2.0)

You can make your document easier to read by changing the amount of space between the lines of text.

## Change Line Spacing

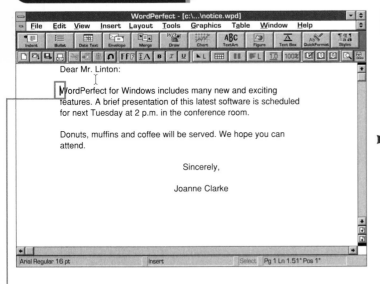

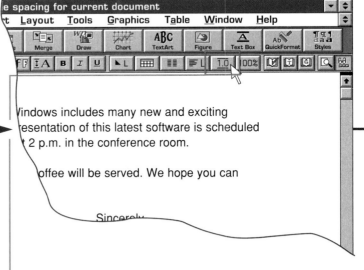

**1** Position the insertion point where you want the new line spacing to begin.

*Note: To change the line spacing of a section of text, select the text you want to change. To select text, refer to page 14.*

**2** Move the mouse ⬚ over `1.0` and then press and hold down the left button.

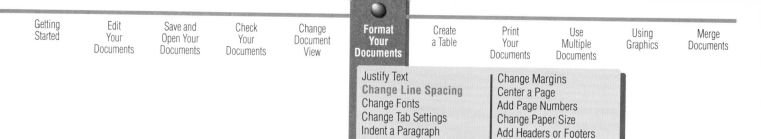

| Getting Started | Edit Your Documents | Save and Open Your Documents | Check Your Documents | Change Document View | **Format Your Documents** | Create a Table | Print Your Documents | Use Multiple Documents | Using Graphics | Merge Documents |

Justify Text
**Change Line Spacing**
Change Fonts
Change Tab Settings
Indent a Paragraph
Add Bullets and Numbers

Change Margins
Center a Page
Add Page Numbers
Change Paper Size
Add Headers or Footers

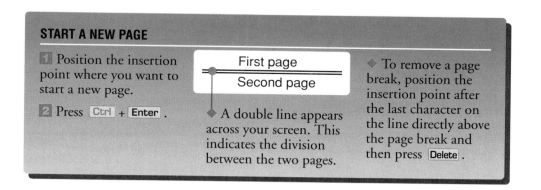

## START A NEW PAGE

**1** Position the insertion point where you want to start a new page.

**2** Press `Ctrl` + `Enter`.

First page
Second page

◆ A double line appears across your screen. This indicates the division between the two pages.

◆ To remove a page break, position the insertion point after the last character on the line directly above the page break and then press `Delete`.

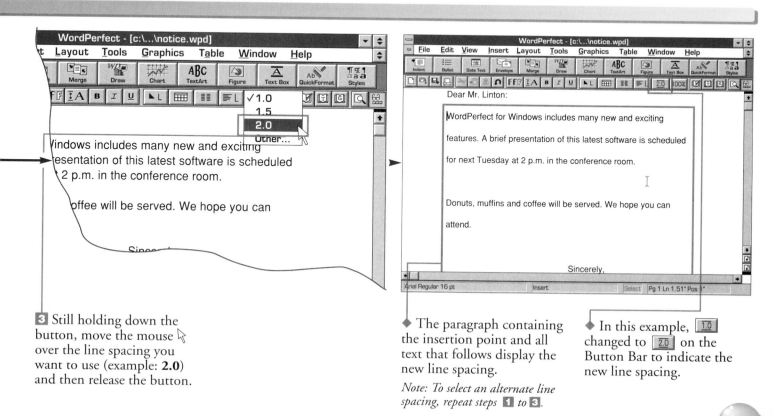

**3** Still holding down the button, move the mouse over the line spacing you want to use (example: **2.0**) and then release the button.

◆ The paragraph containing the insertion point and all text that follows display the new line spacing.

*Note: To select an alternate line spacing, repeat steps **1** to **3**.*

◆ In this example, `1.0` changed to `2.0` on the Button Bar to indicate the new line spacing.

# CHANGE FONTS

You can change the design and size of characters in your document. This enables you to emphasize headings and make text easier to read.

## FFF Change Font Face

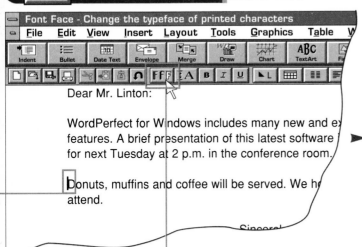

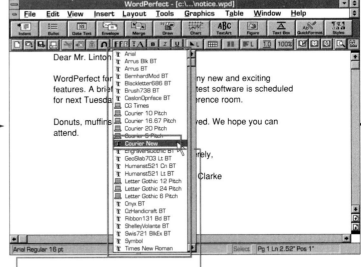

**You can change the font face (design) of text in your document.**

**1** Position the insertion point where you want the new font face to begin.

*Note: To change the font face of a section of text, select the text you want to change. To select text, refer to page 14.*

**2** Move the mouse ↖ over FFF and then press the left button.

◆ A list of the available font faces appears.

**3** Move the mouse ↖ over the font face you want to use (example: **Courier New**) and then press the left button.

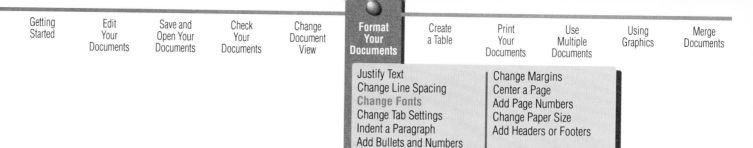

| Getting Started | Edit Your Documents | Save and Open Your Documents | Check Your Documents | Change Document View | **Format Your Documents** | Create a Table | Print Your Documents | Use Multiple Documents | Using Graphics | Merge Documents |

Justify Text
Change Line Spacing
**Change Fonts**
Change Tab Settings
Indent a Paragraph
Add Bullets and Numbers

Change Margins
Center a Page
Add Page Numbers
Change Paper Size
Add Headers or Footers

## BOLD, *ITALIC*, <u>UNDERLINE</u>

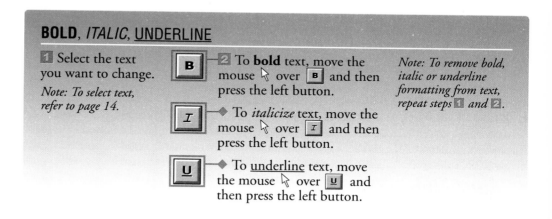

**1** Select the text you want to change.

*Note: To select text, refer to page 14.*

**2** To **bold** text, move the mouse ⌖ over **B** and then press the left button.

◆ To *italicize* text, move the mouse ⌖ over **I** and then press the left button.

◆ To <u>underline</u> text, move the mouse ⌖ over **U** and then press the left button.

*Note: To remove bold, italic or underline formatting from text, repeat steps **1** and **2**.*

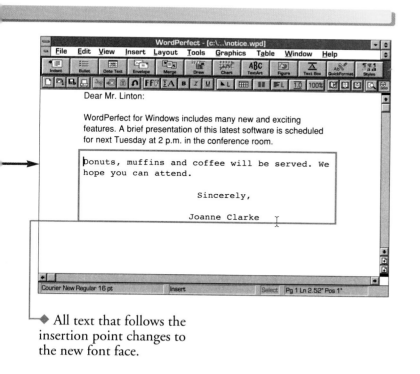

◆ All text that follows the insertion point changes to the new font face.

## CHANGE FONT SIZE

**You can increase or decrease the size of text in your document.**

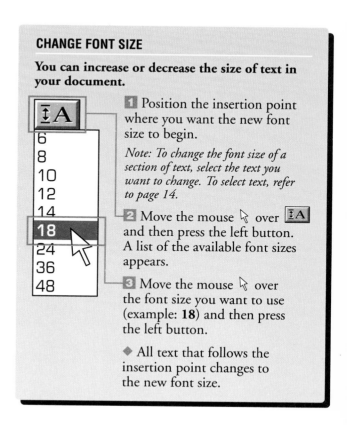

**1** Position the insertion point where you want the new font size to begin.

*Note: To change the font size of a section of text, select the text you want to change. To select text, refer to page 14.*

**2** Move the mouse ⌖ over **IA** and then press the left button. A list of the available font sizes appears.

**3** Move the mouse ⌖ over the font size you want to use (example: **18**) and then press the left button.

◆ All text that follows the insertion point changes to the new font size.

65

# CHANGE FONTS

You can change the design and size of characters in your document at the same time by using the Font dialog box. This enables you to turn a dull and lifeless letter into an interesting, attractive document.

**Change Fonts**

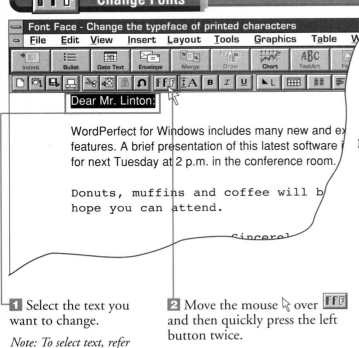

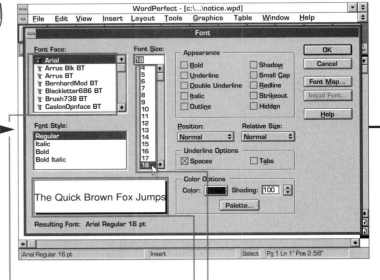

**1** Select the text you want to change.

*Note: To select text, refer to page 14.*

**2** Move the mouse over FFF and then quickly press the left button twice.

◆ The **Font** dialog box appears.

**3** Move the mouse over the font face you want to use (example: **Arial**) and then press the left button.

**4** Move the mouse over the font size you want to use (example: **18**) and then press the left button.

◆ A sample of the font you selected appears.

Justify Text
Change Line Spacing
**Change Fonts**
Change Tab Settings
Indent a Paragraph
Add Bullets and Numbers

Change Margins
Center a Page
Add Page Numbers
Change Paper Size
Add Headers or Footers

◆ The available font faces can vary from one computer to another, depending on the printer and the setup of the computer.

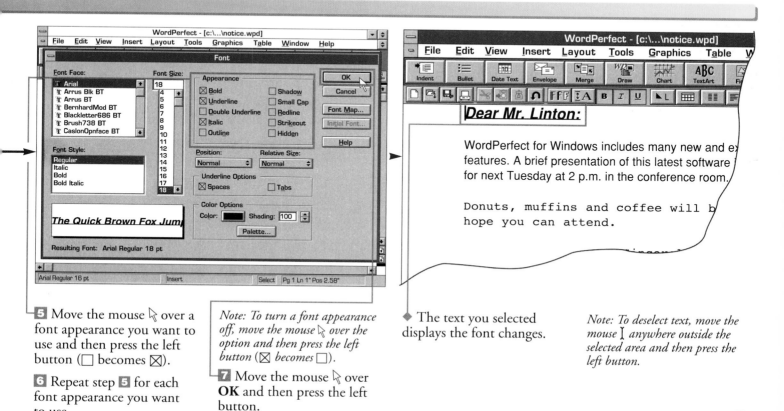

**5** Move the mouse ↳ over a font appearance you want to use and then press the left button (☐ becomes ☒).

**6** Repeat step **5** for each font appearance you want to use.

*Note: To turn a font appearance off, move the mouse ↳ over the option and then press the left button (☒ becomes ☐).*

**7** Move the mouse ↳ over **OK** and then press the left button.

◆ The text you selected displays the font changes.

*Note: To deselect text, move the mouse I anywhere outside the selected area and then press the left button.*

# CHANGE TAB SETTINGS

You can use tabs to line up columns of information in your document.

Make sure you use tabs rather than spaces to line up columns of text. This will ensure your document prints correctly.

| Last Name | First Name | Address | City | State | Zip Code |
|---|---|---|---|---|---|
| Appleton | Jill | 456 John Street | Portland | OR | 97526 |
| DeVries | Monica | 12 Willow Avenue | Los Angeles | CA | 90032 |
| Grossi | Rob | 23 Riverbead Road | Seattle | WA | 98109 |
| Knill | Mark | 97 Speers Road | Denver | CO | 80207 |
| | Justin | 15 Lakeshore Drive | Atlanta | GA | 30367 |
| | Jennifer | 34 Kerr Street | Provo | UT | 84604 |
| | | 56 Devon Road | Dallas | TX | 75236 |

◆ In this example, spaces were used to line up columns.

| Last Name | First Name | Address | City | State | Zip Code |
|---|---|---|---|---|---|
| Appleton | Jill | 456 John Street | Portland | OR | 97526 |
| DeVries | Monica | 12 Willow Avenue | Los Angeles | CA | 90032 |
| Grossi | Rob | 23 Riverbead Road | Seattle | WA | 98109 |
| Knill | Mark | 97 Speers Road | Denver | CO | 80207 |
| Leung | Justin | 15 Lakeshore Drive | Atlanta | GA | 80207 |
| Matwey | Jennifer | 34 Kerr Street | Provo | UT | 84604 |
| Smith | Albert | 56 Devon Road | Dallas | TX | 75236 |
| Smith | Betty | 111 Linton Street | Los Angeles | CA | 90071 |
| Smith | Carol | 36 Ford Drive | Santa Clara | CA | 95054 |
| Anderson | David | 55 Kennedy Road | Buffalo | NY | 14213 |

◆ In this example, tabs were used to line up columns.

## Delete a Tab

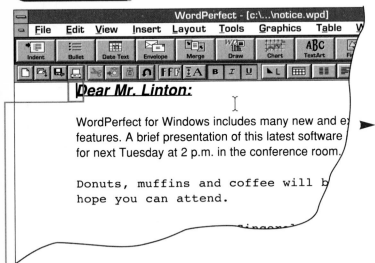

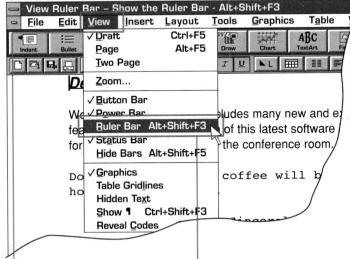

**1** Position the insertion point where you want the new tab settings to begin.

**2** To display the Ruler Bar, move the mouse ⌖ over **View** and then press the left button.

**3** Move the mouse ⌖ over **Ruler Bar** and then press the left button.

*Note: To hide the Ruler Bar, repeat steps **2** and **3**.*

68

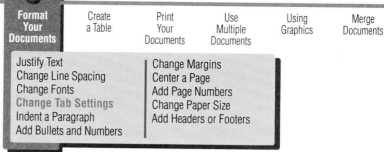

Justify Text
Change Line Spacing
Change Fonts
**Change Tab Settings**
Indent a Paragraph
Add Bullets and Numbers

Change Margins
Center a Page
Add Page Numbers
Change Paper Size
Add Headers or Footers

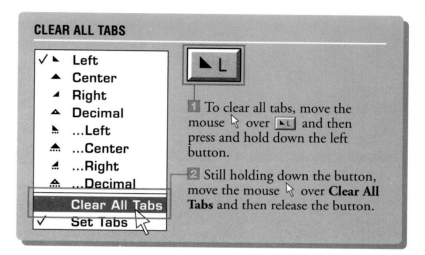

## CLEAR ALL TABS

✓ ◣ Left
◢ Center
◣ Right
◢ Decimal
◣ ...Left
◢ ...Center
◢ ...Right
◢ ...Decimal
**Clear All Tabs**
✓ **Set Tabs**

**1** To clear all tabs, move the mouse over ◣L and then press and hold down the left button.

**2** Still holding down the button, move the mouse over **Clear All Tabs** and then release the button.

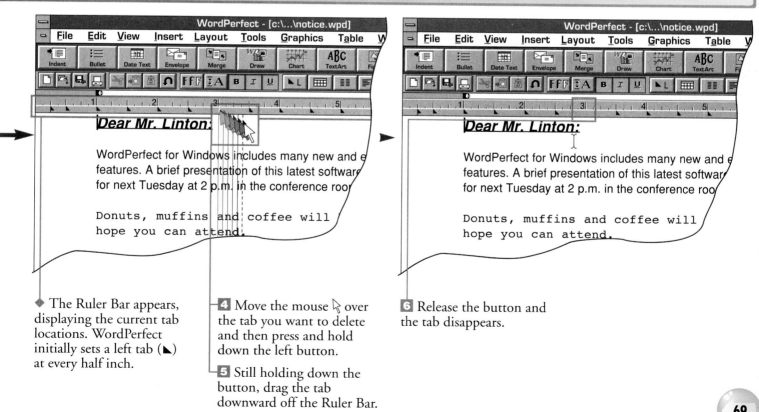

◆ The Ruler Bar appears, displaying the current tab locations. WordPerfect initially sets a left tab (◣) at every half inch.

**4** Move the mouse over the tab you want to delete and then press and hold down the left button.

**5** Still holding down the button, drag the tab downward off the Ruler Bar.

**6** Release the button and the tab disappears.

69

WordPerfect offers four types of tabs to help you line up text in your document.

**Left tab**
**Right tab**
**Center tab**
**123.45** (Decimal tab)

Tab position

## Add a Tab

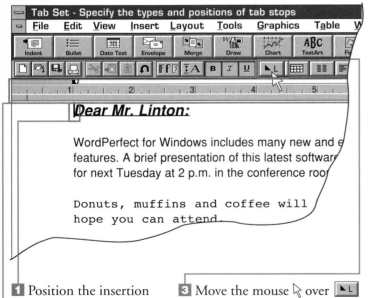

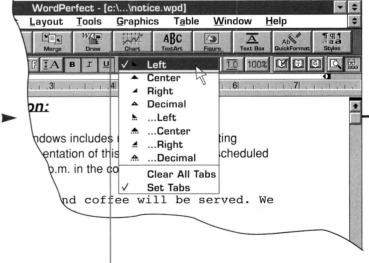

**1** Position the insertion point where you want the new tab settings to begin.

**2** Display the Ruler Bar.

*Note: To display the Ruler Bar, perform steps 2 and 3 on page 68.*

**3** Move the mouse ⌖ over ▲L and then press and hold down the left button.

**4** Still holding down the button, move the mouse ⌖ over the tab you want to use (example: **Left**) and then release the button.

Justify Text
Change Line Spacing
Change Fonts
**Change Tab Settings**
Indent a Paragraph
Add Bullets and Numbers

Change Margins
Center a Page
Add Page Numbers
Change Paper Size
Add Headers or Footers

You can insert a row of dots before a tab to help lead the eye from one column of information to another. This is very useful if you want to create a Table of Contents.

**Left tab**
**Right tab**
**Center tab**
**123.45** (Decimal tab)

Tab position

**Using Tabs**

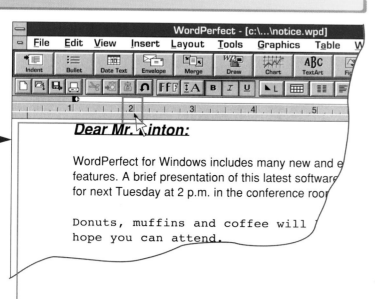

**5** Move the mouse ↕ over the position on the Ruler Bar where you want to add the tab and then press the left button.

◆ The new tab setting appears on the Ruler Bar.

*Note: To hide the Ruler Bar, perform steps **2** and **3** on page 68.*

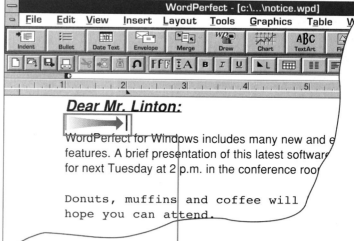

**After you have set the tabs, you can use them to quickly move the insertion point across your screen.**

**1** Position the insertion point at the beginning of the line you want to move the insertion point across.

**2** Press **Tab** and the insertion point moves to the first tab stop.

71

# INDENT A PARAGRAPH

- ◆ Indent
- ◆ Double Indent
- ◆ Hanging Indent

You can emphasize paragraphs in your document by indenting them.

## Indent a Paragraph

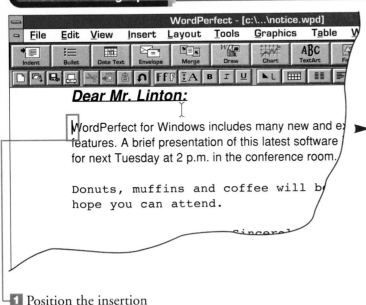

**1** Position the insertion point in front of the first character of the paragraph you want to indent.

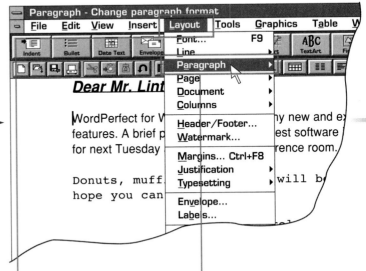

**2** Move the mouse ⬡ over **Layout** and then press the left button.

**3** Move the mouse ⬡ over **Paragraph** and then press the left button.

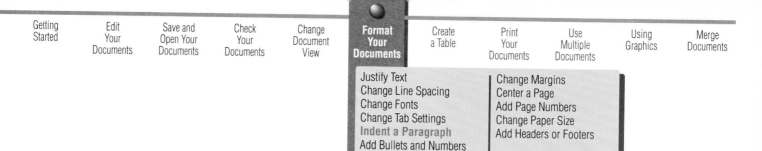

Justify Text
Change Line Spacing
Change Fonts
Change Tab Settings
Indent a Paragraph
Add Bullets and Numbers

Change Margins
Center a Page
Add Page Numbers
Change Paper Size
Add Headers or Footers

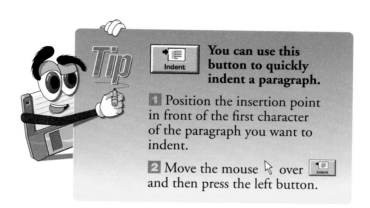

*Tip*

**You can use this button to quickly indent a paragraph.**

**1** Position the insertion point in front of the first character of the paragraph you want to indent.

**2** Move the mouse ⌖ over [Indent] and then press the left button.

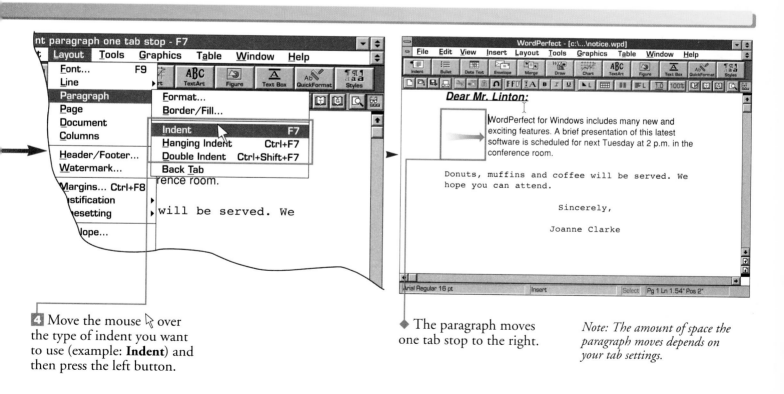

**4** Move the mouse ⌖ over the type of indent you want to use (example: **Indent**) and then press the left button.

◆ The paragraph moves one tab stop to the right.

*Note: The amount of space the paragraph moves depends on your tab settings.*

# ADD BULLETS AND NUMBERS

> You can emphasize text in a list by beginning each item with a bullet or number. WordPerfect offers several bullet and number styles that you can choose from.

## Add Bullets and Numbers

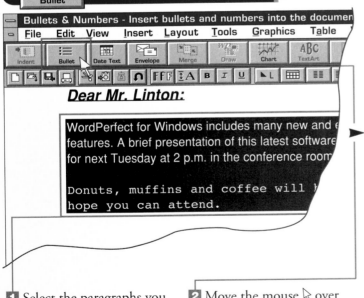

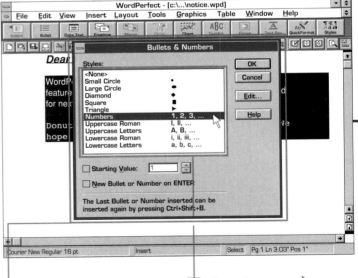

**1** Select the paragraphs you want to display bullets or numbers.

**2** Move the mouse over **Bullet** and then press the left button.

◆ The **Bullets & Numbers** dialog box appears.

**3** Move the mouse over the style you want to use (example: **Numbers**) and then press the left button.

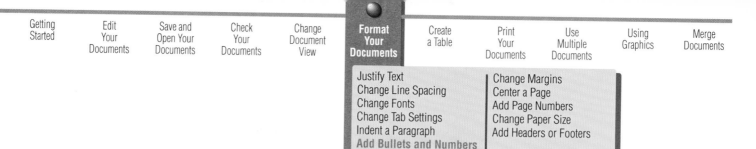

Justify Text · Change Margins
Change Line Spacing · Center a Page
Change Fonts · Add Page Numbers
Change Tab Settings · Change Paper Size
Indent a Paragraph · Add Headers or Footers
**Add Bullets and Numbers**

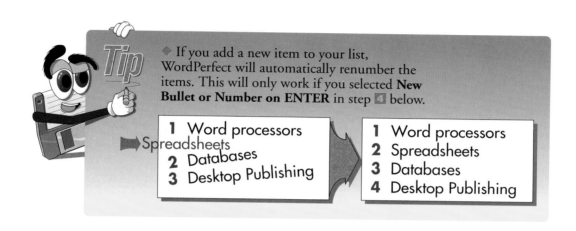

◆ If you add a new item to your list, WordPerfect will automatically renumber the items. This will only work if you selected **New Bullet or Number on ENTER** in step **4** below.

Spreadsheets

1 Word processors
2 Databases
3 Desktop Publishing

1 Word processors
2 Spreadsheets
3 Databases
4 Desktop Publishing

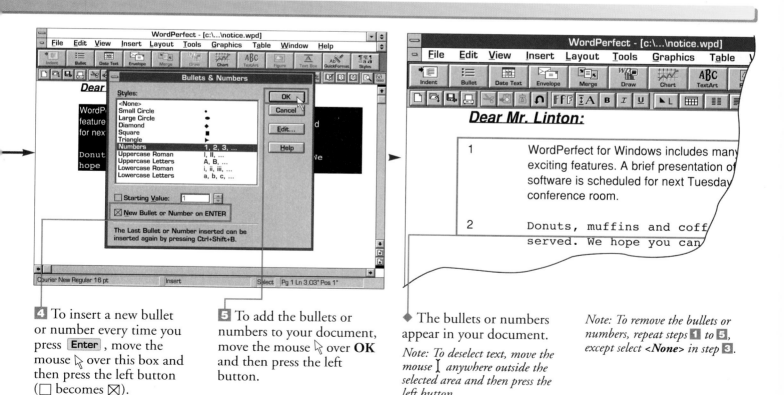

**4** To insert a new bullet or number every time you press **Enter** , move the mouse ▷ over this box and then press the left button (☐ becomes ☒).

**5** To add the bullets or numbers to your document, move the mouse ▷ over **OK** and then press the left button.

◆ The bullets or numbers appear in your document.

*Note: To deselect text, move the mouse I anywhere outside the selected area and then press the left button.*

*Note: To remove the bullets or numbers, repeat steps **1** to **5**, except select* ***<None>*** *in step **3**.*

75

# CHANGE MARGINS

When you create a document, WordPerfect automatically sets the left and right margins at one inch. You can change these settings to shorten or lengthen the size of your document.

A margin is the space between the text and the edge of your paper.

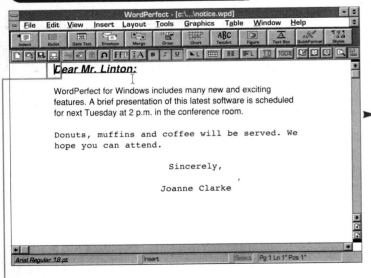

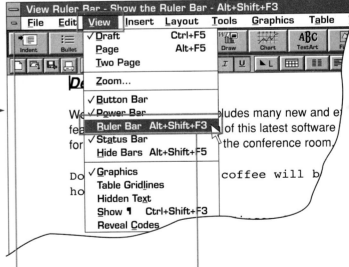

**1** Position the insertion point where you want the new margin(s) to begin.

*Note: To change the margin(s) of a section of text, select the text you want to change. To select text, refer to page 14.*

*To change the top and bottom margins, refer to page 78.*

**2** To display the Ruler Bar, move the mouse ⌖ over **View** and then press the left button.

**3** Move the mouse ⌖ over **Ruler Bar** and then press the left button.

Justify Text
Change Line Spacing
Change Fonts
Change Tab Settings
Indent a Paragraph
Add Bullets and Numbers

**Change Margins**
Center a Page
Add Page Numbers
Change Paper Size
Add Headers or Footers

## MARGIN MARKERS

The Ruler Bar displays the margin markers. These markers indicate the current positions of the left and right margins and enable you to change them.

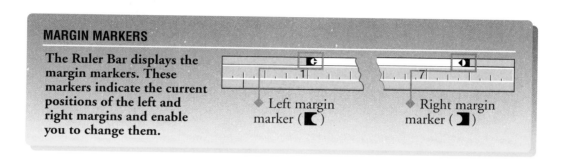

◆ Left margin marker (◖)　　◆ Right margin marker (◗)

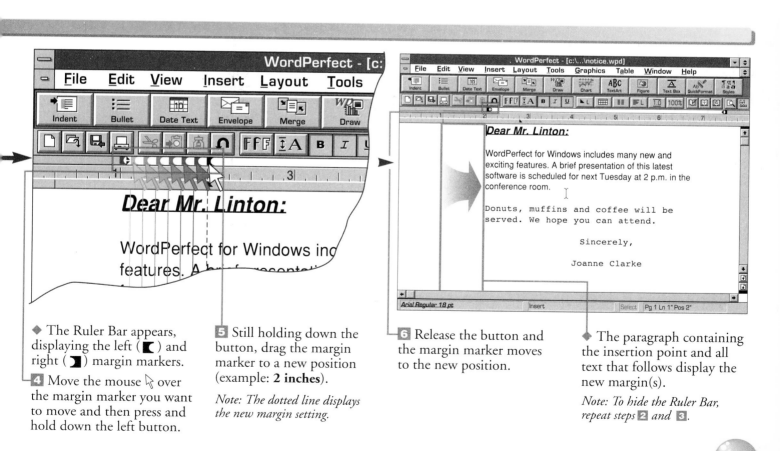

◆ The Ruler Bar appears, displaying the left (◖) and right (◗) margin markers.

**4** Move the mouse ⬚ over the margin marker you want to move and then press and hold down the left button.

**5** Still holding down the button, drag the margin marker to a new position (example: **2 inches**).

*Note: The dotted line displays the new margin setting.*

**6** Release the button and the margin marker moves to the new position.

◆ The paragraph containing the insertion point and all text that follows display the new margin(s).

*Note: To hide the Ruler Bar, repeat steps **2** and **3**.*

# CHANGE MARGINS

WordPerfect automatically sets the top and bottom margins in your document at one inch. You can change these settings to accommodate letterhead or other specialty papers.

A margin is the space between the text and the edge of your paper.

## Change Top and Bottom Margins

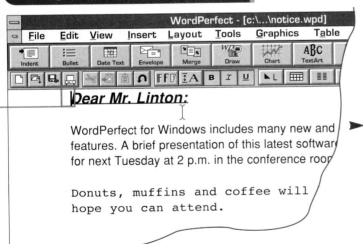

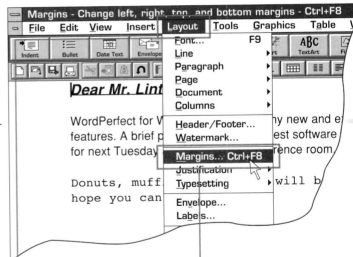

**1** Position the insertion point anywhere in the page where you want the new margin(s) to begin.

**2** Move the mouse ⌖ over **Layout** and then press the left button.

**3** Move the mouse ⌖ over **Margins** and then press the left button.

Justify Text
Change Line Spacing
Change Fonts
Change Tab Settings
Indent a Paragraph
Add Bullets and Numbers

**Change Margins**
Center a Page
Add Page Numbers
Change Paper Size
Add Headers or Footers

**Top and bottom margins will not appear on your screen when you are in the Draft mode.**

**To view the margins, you can use** 🔍 **to display an entire page.**

1 Move the mouse ⇖ over 🔍 and then press the left button.

*Note: Repeat step 1 to return to the original view.*

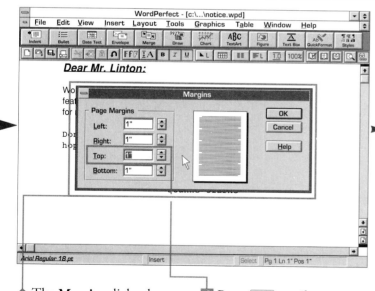

◆ The **Margins** dialog box appears.

*Note: You can use this dialog box to change the left, right, top and bottom margins.*

4 Press **Tab** until you highlight the number beside the margin you want to change (example: **Top**).

5 Type the new margin in inches (example: **2**).

*Note: Repeat steps 4 and 5 for each margin you want to change.*

6 Move the mouse ⇖ over **OK** and then press the left button.

◆ The page containing the insertion point and all pages that follow will change to the new margin(s).

You can vertically center text on a page. This is useful when creating title pages or short memos.

## Center a Page

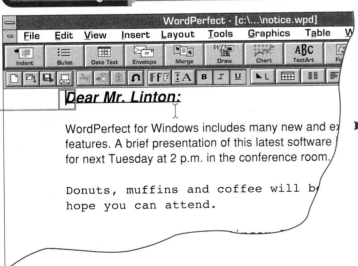

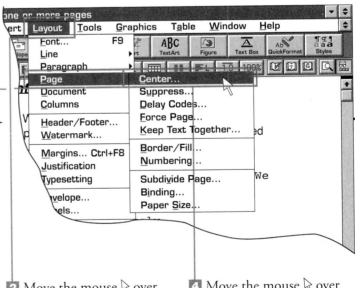

**1** Position the insertion point anywhere on the page you want to vertically center.

**2** Move the mouse ℝ over **Layout** and then press the left button.

**3** Move the mouse ℝ over **Page** and then press the left button.

**4** Move the mouse ℝ over **Center** and then press the left button.

Justify Text  
Change Line Spacing  
Change Fonts  
Change Tab Settings  
Indent a Paragraph  
Add Bullets and Numbers

Change Margins  
**Center a Page**  
Add Page Numbers  
Change Paper Size  
Add Headers or Footers

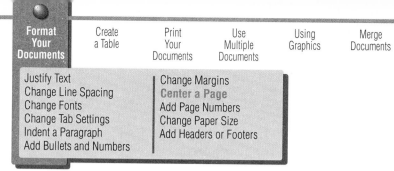

You can use 🔍 to display an entire page. This will enable you to view the page you centered.

1 Move the mouse ⌖ over 🔍 and then press the left button.

*Note: Repeat step 1 to return to the original view.*

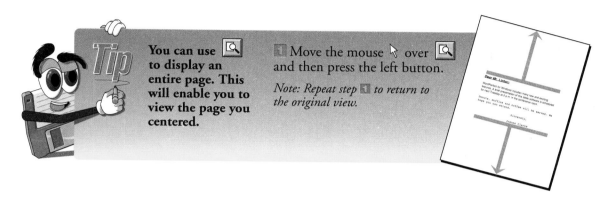

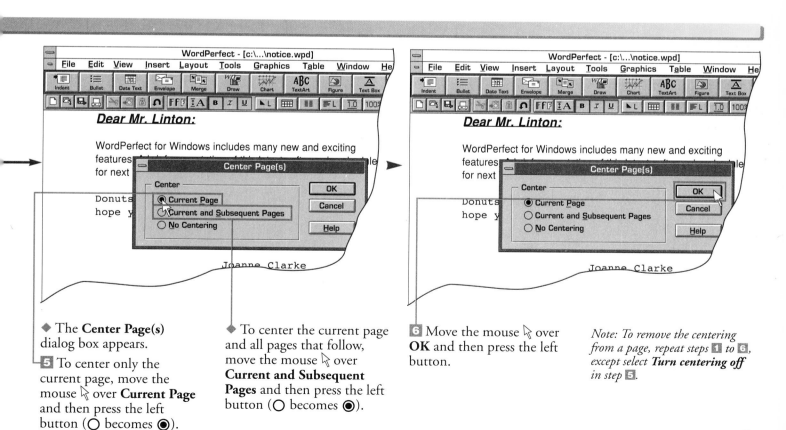

◆ The **Center Page(s)** dialog box appears.

5 To center only the current page, move the mouse ⌖ over **Current Page** and then press the left button (○ becomes ●).

◆ To center the current page and all pages that follow, move the mouse ⌖ over **Current and Subsequent Pages** and then press the left button (○ becomes ●).

6 Move the mouse ⌖ over **OK** and then press the left button.

*Note: To remove the centering from a page, repeat steps 1 to 6, except select* ***Turn centering off*** *in step 5.*

# ADD PAGE NUMBERS

You can have WordPerfect automatically number the pages in your document.

## Add Page Numbers

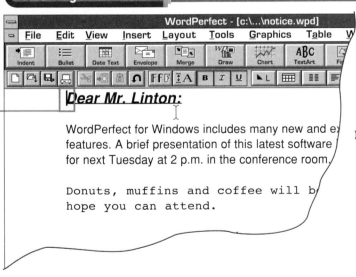

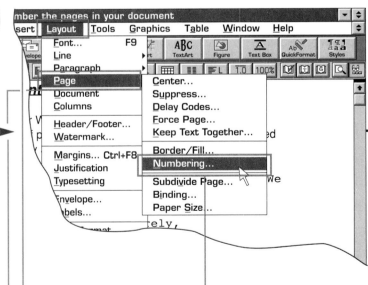

**1** Position the insertion point anywhere on the page where you want the numbering to begin.

**2** Move the mouse over **Layout** and then press the left button.

**3** Move the mouse over **Page** and then press the left button.

**4** Move the mouse over **Numbering** and then press the left button.

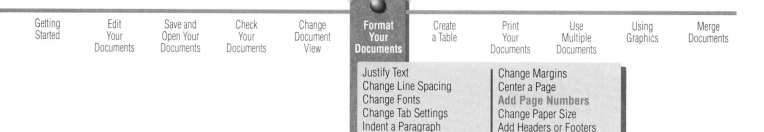

Justify Text
Change Line Spacing
Change Fonts
Change Tab Settings
Indent a Paragraph
Add Bullets and Numbers

Change Margins
Center a Page
**Add Page Numbers**
Change Paper Size
Add Headers or Footers

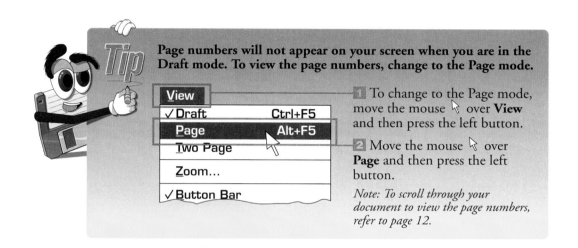

**Page numbers will not appear on your screen when you are in the Draft mode. To view the page numbers, change to the Page mode.**

View
✓ Draft          Ctrl+F5
Page             Alt+F5
Two Page
Zoom...
✓ Button Bar

**1** To change to the Page mode, move the mouse ⌖ over **View** and then press the left button.

**2** Move the mouse ⌖ over **Page** and then press the left button.

*Note: To scroll through your document to view the page numbers, refer to page 12.*

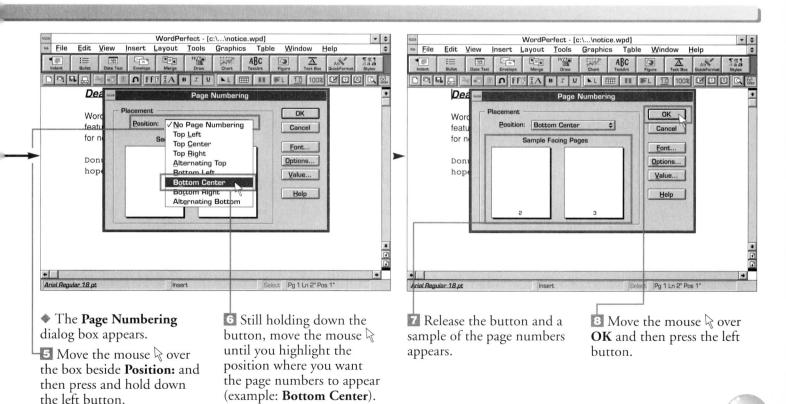

◆ The **Page Numbering** dialog box appears.

**5** Move the mouse ⌖ over the box beside **Position:** and then press and hold down the left button.

**6** Still holding down the button, move the mouse ⌖ until you highlight the position where you want the page numbers to appear (example: **Bottom Center**).

**7** Release the button and a sample of the page numbers appears.

**8** Move the mouse ⌖ over **OK** and then press the left button.

# CHANGE PAPER SIZE

> WordPerfect automatically sets each page in your document to print on 8.5 by 11 inch paper. If you want to use a different paper size, you can change this setting.

## Change Paper Size

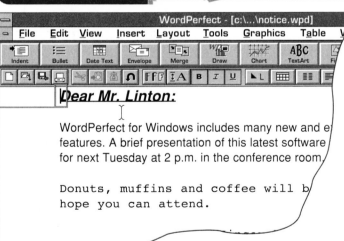

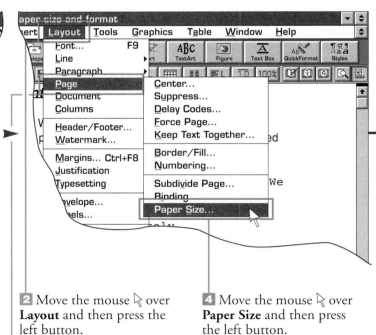

**1** Position the insertion point anywhere in the first page you want to print using the new paper size.

**2** Move the mouse ⌖ over **Layout** and then press the left button.

**3** Move the mouse ⌖ over **Page** and then press the left button.

**4** Move the mouse ⌖ over **Paper Size** and then press the left button.

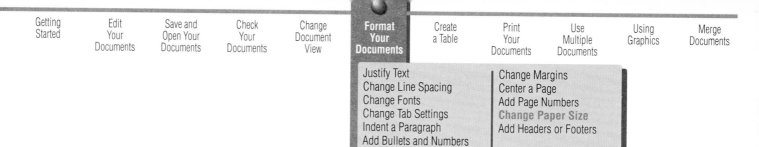

# Getting Started / Edit Your Documents / Save and Open Your Documents / Check Your Documents / Change Document View / **Format Your Documents** / Create a Table / Print Your Documents / Use Multiple Documents / Using Graphics / Merge Documents

Justify Text      Change Margins
Change Line Spacing      Center a Page
Change Fonts      Add Page Numbers
Change Tab Settings      **Change Paper Size**
Indent a Paragraph      Add Headers or Footers
Add Bullets and Numbers

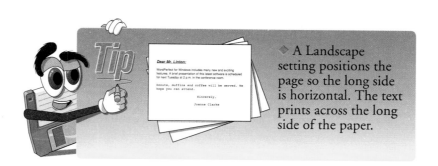

◆ A Landscape setting positions the page so the long side is horizontal. The text prints across the long side of the paper.

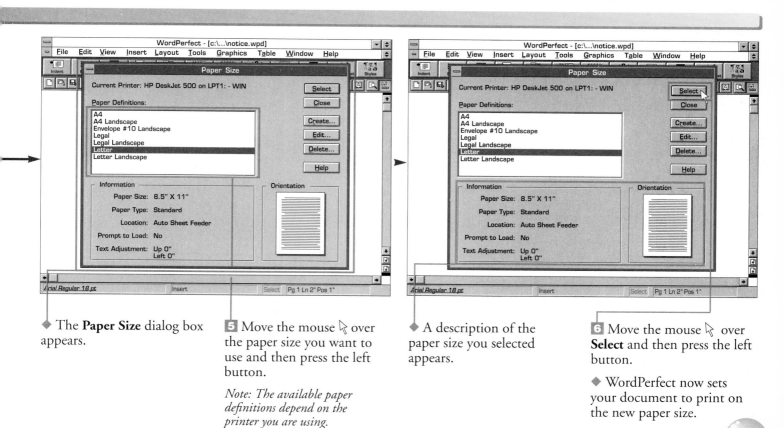

◆ The **Paper Size** dialog box appears.

**5** Move the mouse � over the paper size you want to use and then press the left button.

*Note: The available paper definitions depend on the printer you are using.*

◆ A description of the paper size you selected appears.

**6** Move the mouse � over **Select** and then press the left button.

◆ WordPerfect now sets your document to print on the new paper size.

85

# ADD HEADERS OR FOOTERS

You can use headers and footers to print information on each page or on alternating pages in your document. This information may include the title of your document, the date or your company name.

**◆ Header**
A Header appears at the top of a page.

**◆ Footer**
A Footer appears at the bottom of a page.

## Add Headers or Footers

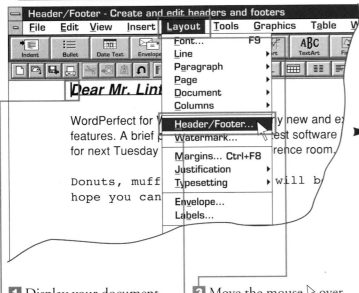

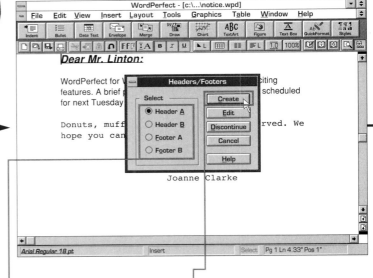

**1** Display your document in the Page mode.

**2** Position the insertion point at the top of the first page you want to include the header or footer.

**3** Move the mouse ⇱ over **Layout** and then press the left button.

**4** Move the mouse ⇱ over **Header/Footer** and then press the left button.

**◆** The **Headers/Footers** dialog box appears.

**5** Move the mouse ⇱ over the header or footer you want to create (example: **Header A**) and then press the left button.

*Note: You can create two headers and two footers (**A** and **B**) for each page.*

**6** Move the mouse ⇱ over **Create** and then press the left button.

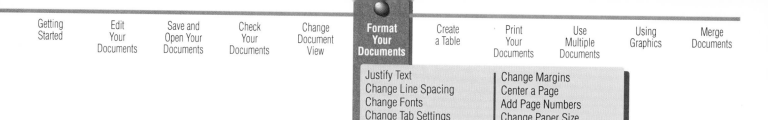

| Getting Started | Edit Your Documents | Save and Open Your Documents | Check Your Documents | Change Document View | **Format Your Documents** | Create a Table | Print Your Documents | Use Multiple Documents | Using Graphics | Merge Documents |

Justify Text
Change Line Spacing
Change Fonts
Change Tab Settings
Indent a Paragraph
Add Bullets and Numbers

Change Margins
Center a Page
Add Page Numbers
Change Paper Size
**Add Headers or Footers**

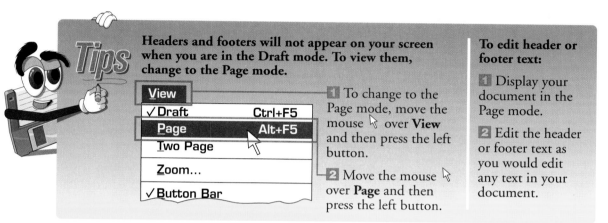

**Headers and footers will not appear on your screen when you are in the Draft mode. To view them, change to the Page mode.**

| View | |
|---|---|
| ✓Draft | Ctrl+F5 |
| Page | Alt+F5 |
| Two Page | |
| Zoom... | |
| ✓Button Bar | |

**1** To change to the Page mode, move the mouse over **View** and then press the left button.

**2** Move the mouse over **Page** and then press the left button.

**To edit header or footer text:**

**1** Display your document in the Page mode.

**2** Edit the header or footer text as you would edit any text in your document.

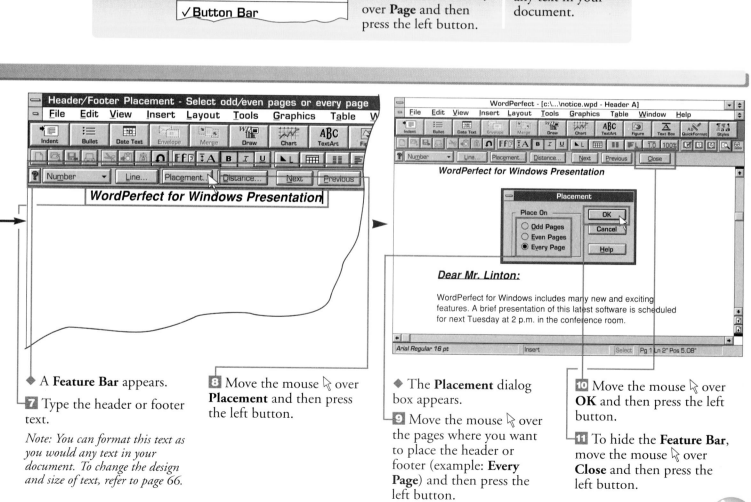

◆ A **Feature Bar** appears.

**7** Type the header or footer text.

*Note: You can format this text as you would any text in your document. To change the design and size of text, refer to page 66.*

**8** Move the mouse over **Placement** and then press the left button.

◆ The **Placement** dialog box appears.

**9** Move the mouse over the pages where you want to place the header or footer (example: **Every Page**) and then press the left button.

**10** Move the mouse over **OK** and then press the left button.

**11** To hide the **Feature Bar**, move the mouse over **Close** and then press the left button.

87

You can create a table to organize your information. A table consists of rows, columns and cells.

Tap Tap Tap

**Column**
A column is a vertical line of boxes.

**Row**
A row is a horizontal line of boxes.

**Cell**
A cell is the area where a row and column intersect.

### Create a Table

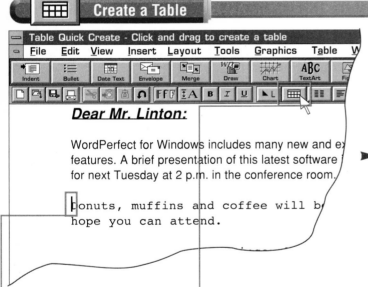

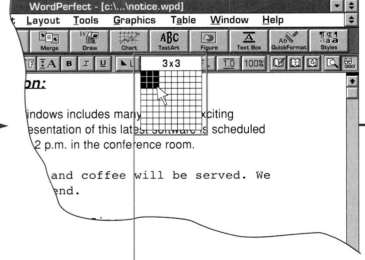

**1** To create a table, position the insertion point where you want the table to appear in your document.

**2** Move the mouse ⌖ over 📅 .

**3** Press and hold down the left button as you move the mouse ⌖ over the table size you want to create (example: **3x3**).

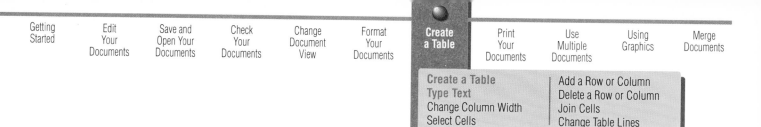

**Create a Table**
**Type Text**
Change Column Width
Select Cells

Add a Row or Column
Delete a Row or Column
Join Cells
Change Table Lines

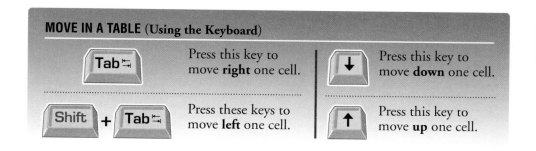

**MOVE IN A TABLE** (Using the Keyboard)

| | |
|---|---|
| **Tab** — Press this key to move **right** one cell. | **↓** — Press this key to move **down** one cell. |
| **Shift** + **Tab** — Press these keys to move **left** one cell. | **↑** — Press this key to move **up** one cell. |

## Type Text

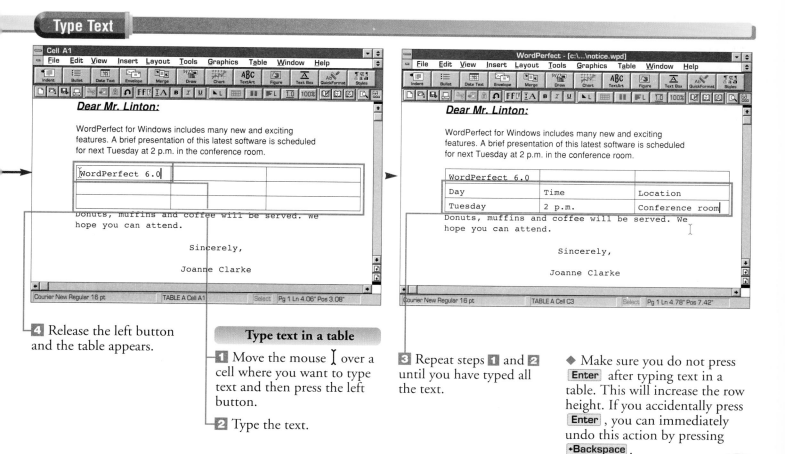

**4** Release the left button and the table appears.

### Type text in a table

**1** Move the mouse I over a cell where you want to type text and then press the left button.

**2** Type the text.

**3** Repeat steps **1** and **2** until you have typed all the text.

◆ Make sure you do not press **Enter** after typing text in a table. This will increase the row height. If you accidentally press **Enter**, you can immediately undo this action by pressing **+Backspace**.

89

> You can adjust the columns in your table to make them wider or narrower.

## Change Column Width

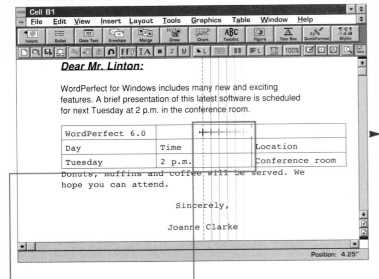

**1** Move the mouse I over the left or right edge of the column you want to change and I becomes ✛.

**2** Press and hold down the left button as you drag the edge of the column to a new position.

◆ The dotted line indicates the new position.

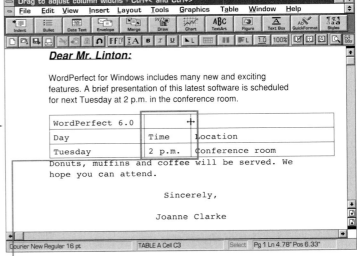

**3** Release the button and the new column width appears.

When making changes to your table, you may have to select the cells you want to modify. Selected cells appear highlighted on your screen.

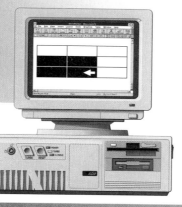

## Select Cells

### To select a cell

**1** Move the mouse I over the left edge of the cell ( I becomes ⇦ ) and then press the left button.

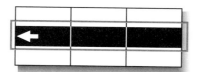

### To select a row

**1** Move the mouse I over the left edge of any cell in the row ( I becomes ⇦ ) and then quickly press the left button twice.

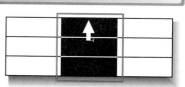

### To select a column

**1** Move the mouse I over the top edge of any cell in the column ( I becomes ⇧ ) and then quickly press the left button twice.

### To select an entire table

**1** Move the mouse I over the left edge of any cell in the table ( I becomes ⇦ ) and then quickly press the left button three times.

### To select several cells

**1** Move the mouse I over the first cell you want to select and then press and hold down the left button.

**2** Still holding down the button, move the mouse ⇦ until you highlight all the cells you want to select. Then release the button.

### To deselect cells

**1** Move the mouse I anywhere outside the table and then press the left button.

You can insert a row or column to your table if you want to add new information.

## Add a Row or Column

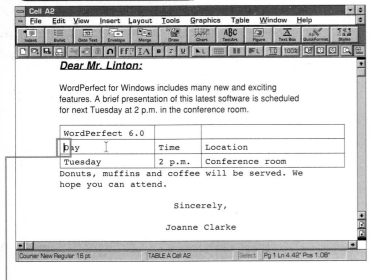

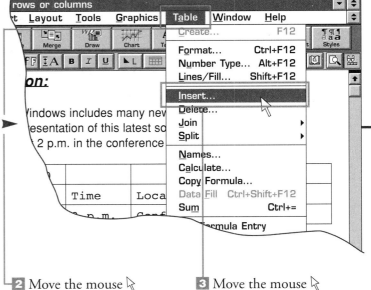

**1** Position the insertion point where you want to add a row or column.

*Note: When you add a row, the row containing the insertion point moves down.*

*When you add a column, the column containing the insertion point moves to the right.*

**2** Move the mouse ⌖ over **Table** and then press the left button.

**3** Move the mouse ⌖ over **Insert** and then press the left button.

Create a Table
Type Text
Change Column Width
Select Cells

**Add a Row or Column**
Delete a Row or Column
Join Cells
Change Table Lines

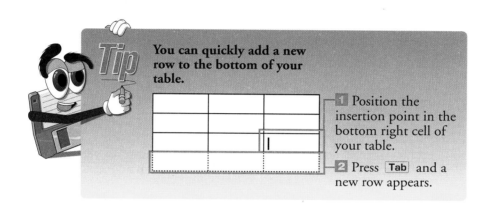

*Tip*

**You can quickly add a new row to the bottom of your table.**

**1** Position the insertion point in the bottom right cell of your table.

**2** Press `Tab` and a new row appears.

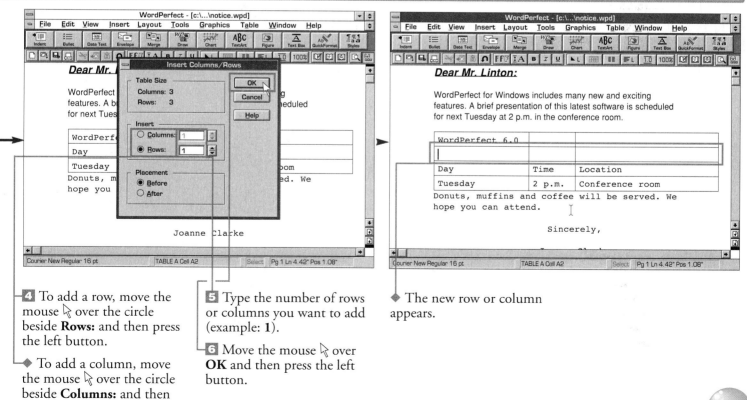

**4** To add a row, move the mouse ⬧ over the circle beside **Rows:** and then press the left button.

◆ To add a column, move the mouse ⬧ over the circle beside **Columns:** and then press the left button.

**5** Type the number of rows or columns you want to add (example: **1**).

**6** Move the mouse ⬧ over **OK** and then press the left button.

◆ The new row or column appears.

93

# DELETE A ROW OR COLUMN

You can delete a row or column from your table. This allows you to remove information or extra cells you no longer require.

## Delete a Row or Column

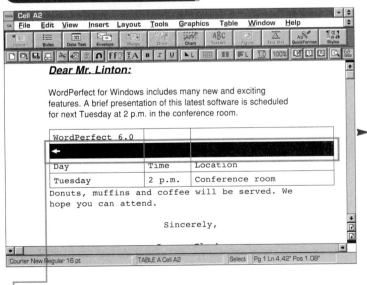

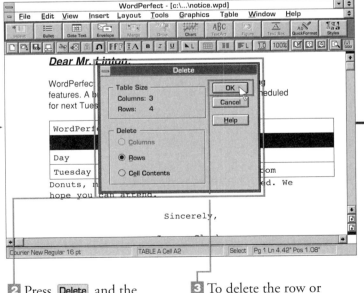

**1** Select the row or column you want to delete.

*Note: To select a row or column, refer to page 91.*

**2** Press `Delete` and the **Delete** dialog box appears.

**3** To delete the row or column you selected, move the mouse ⬚ over **OK** and then press the left button.

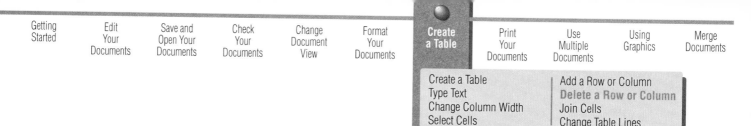

Create a Table
Type Text
Change Column Width
Select Cells

Add a Row or Column
**Delete a Row or Column**
Join Cells
Change Table Lines

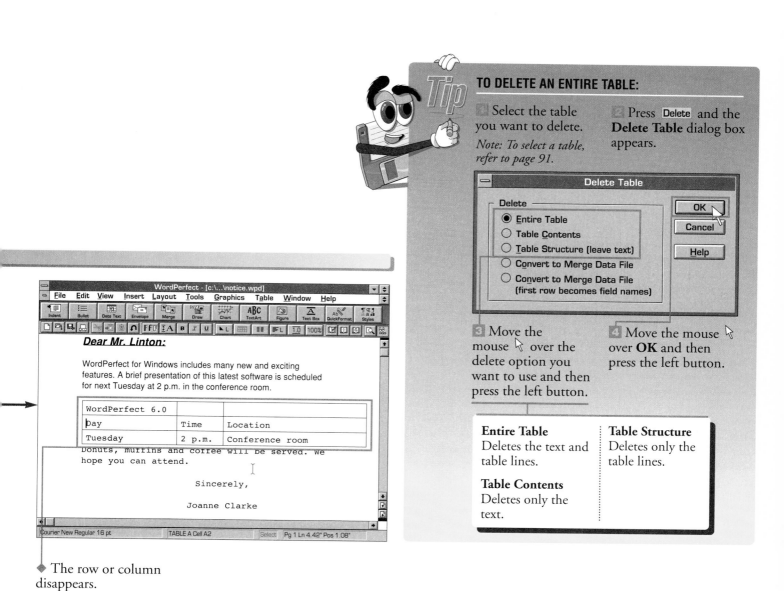

### TO DELETE AN ENTIRE TABLE:

Select the table you want to delete.

*Note: To select a table, refer to page 91.*

Press Delete and the **Delete Table** dialog box appears.

**Delete Table**

**Delete**
- ● **Entire Table**
- ○ **Table Contents**
- ○ **Table Structure (leave text)**
- ○ **Convert to Merge Data File**
- ○ **Convert to Merge Data File (first row becomes field names)**

OK
Cancel
Help

3 Move the mouse over the delete option you want to use and then press the left button.

4 Move the mouse over **OK** and then press the left button.

**Entire Table**
Deletes the text and table lines.

**Table Structure**
Deletes only the table lines.

**Table Contents**
Deletes only the text.

---

**Dear Mr. Linton:**

WordPerfect for Windows includes many new and exciting features. A brief presentation of this latest software is scheduled for next Tuesday at 2 p.m. in the conference room.

| WordPerfect 6.0 | | |
|---|---|---|
| Day | Time | Location |
| Tuesday | 2 p.m. | Conference room |

Donuts, muffins and coffee will be served. We hope you can attend.

Sincerely,

Joanne Clarke

Courier New Regular 16 pt     TABLE A Cell A2     Select   Pg 1 Ln 4.42" Pos 1.08"

◆ The row or column disappears.

*WordPerfect allows you to combine two or more cells in your table to make one large cell. This is useful if you want to display a title at the top of your table.*

## Join Cells

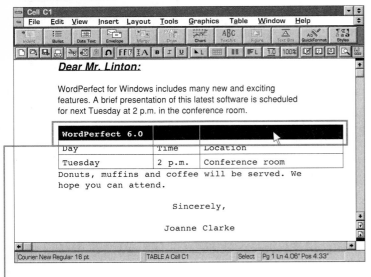

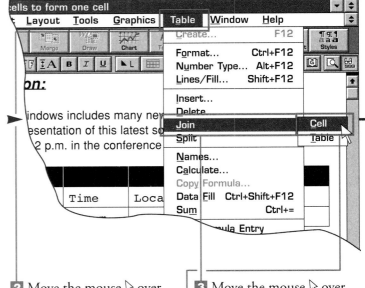

**1** Select the cells in your table you want to join together.

*Note: To select cells, refer to page 91.*

**2** Move the mouse ⌖ over **Table** and then press the left button.

**3** Move the mouse ⌖ over **Join** and then press the left button.

**4** Move the mouse ⌖ over **Cell** and then press the left button.

Create a Table
Type Text
Change Column Width
Select Cells

Add a Row or Column
Delete a Row or Column
*Join Cells*
Change Table Lines

## SPLIT CELLS

**You can split one cell into two or more cells.**

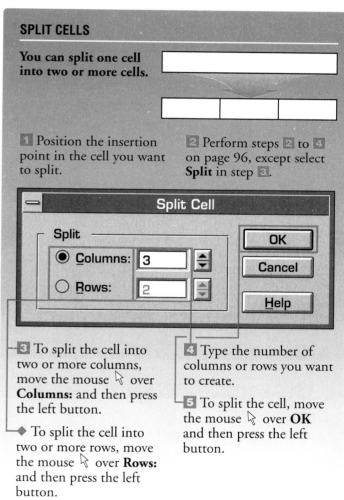

**1** Position the insertion point in the cell you want to split.

**2** Perform steps **2** to **4** on page 96, except select **Split** in step **3**.

**3** To split the cell into two or more columns, move the mouse ▷ over **Columns:** and then press the left button.

◆ To split the cell into two or more rows, move the mouse ▷ over **Rows:** and then press the left button.

**4** Type the number of columns or rows you want to create.

**5** To split the cell, move the mouse ▷ over **OK** and then press the left button.

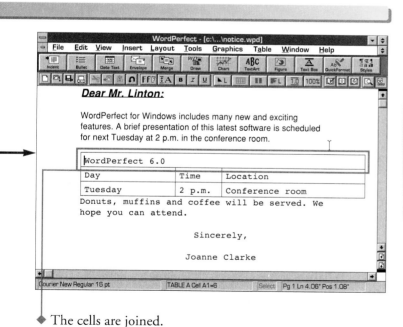

◆ The cells are joined.

# CHANGE TABLE LINES

You can emphasize information and enhance the appearance of your table by making changes to the table lines. WordPerfect offers several types of lines you can choose from.

## Change Table Lines

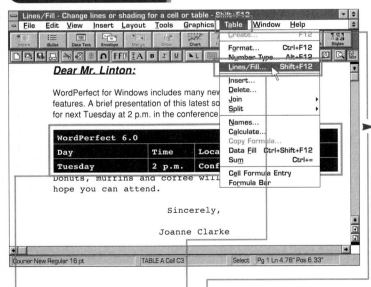

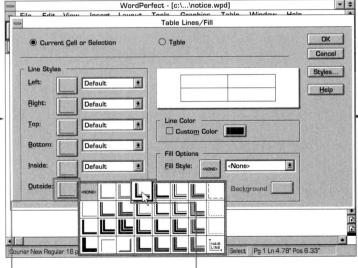

**1** Select the cells in your table that contain the lines you want to change.

*Note: To select cells, refer to page 91.*

**2** Move the mouse ⊠ over **Table** and then press the left button.

**3** Move the mouse ⊠ over **Lines/Fill** and then press the left button.

**4** Move the mouse ⊠ over the box beside the line you want to change (example: **Outside**) and then press the left button.

◆ A list of the available line styles appears.

**5** Move the mouse ⊠ over the line style you want to use and then press the left button.

*Note: Repeat steps **4** and **5** for each line you want to change.*

Create a Table
Type Text
Change Column Width
Select Cells

Add a Row or Column
Delete a Row or Column
Join Cells
**Change Table Lines**

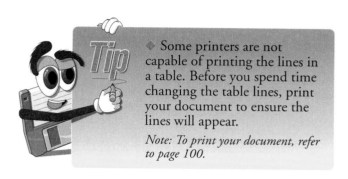

◆ Some printers are not capable of printing the lines in a table. Before you spend time changing the table lines, print your document to ensure the lines will appear.

*Note: To print your document, refer to page 100.*

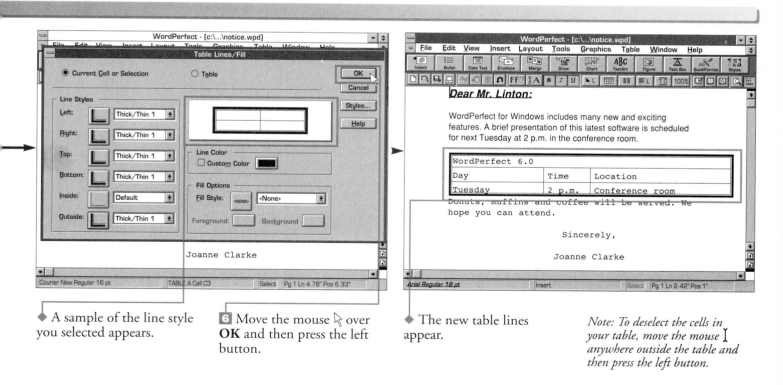

◆ A sample of the line style you selected appears.

**6** Move the mouse � over **OK** and then press the left button.

◆ The new table lines appear.

*Note: To deselect the cells in your table, move the mouse I anywhere outside the table and then press the left button.*

# PRINT A
# DOCUMENT

You can print a single page, specific pages or your entire document.

---

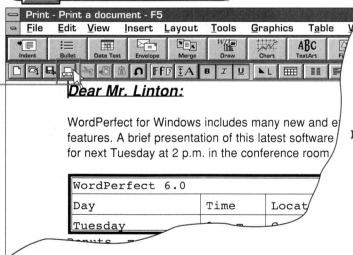

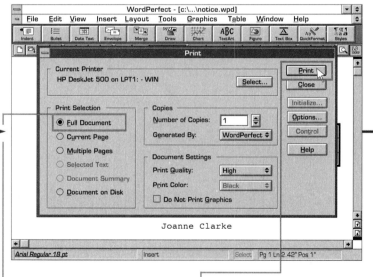

**1** Move the mouse ▷ over 🖨 and then press the left button.

*Note: To print a small section of text in your document, select the text you want to print before performing step **1**. To select text, refer to page 14.*

◆ The **Print** dialog box appears.

**2** Move the mouse ▷ over the print selection you want to use (example: **Full Document**) and then press the left button.

**3** Move the mouse ▷ over **Print** and then press the left button.

| Getting Started | Edit Your Documents | Save and Open Your Documents | Check Your Documents | Change Document View | Format Your Documents | Create a Table | Print Your Documents | Use Multiple Documents | Using Graphics | Merge Documents |

**Print a Document**
Print an Envelope

## PRINT SELECTION

**Full Document**
Prints every page in your document.

**Current Page**
Prints the page containing the insertion point.

**Multiple Pages**
Prints the pages you specify in your document.

**Selected Text**
Prints text you select in your document.

---

*WordPerfect for Windows Presentation*

**_Dear Mr. Linton:_**

WordPerfect for Windows includes many new and exciting features. A brief presentation of this latest software is scheduled for next Tuesday at 2 p.m. in the conference room.

| WordPerfect 6.0 | | |
|---|---|---|
| Day | Time | Location |
| Tuesday | 2 p.m. | Conference room |

Donuts, muffins and coffee will be served. We hope you can attend.

Sincerely,

Joanne Clarke

1

## PRINT MULTIPLE PAGES

Repeat steps **1** to **3** on page 100, except select **Multiple Pages** in step **2**.

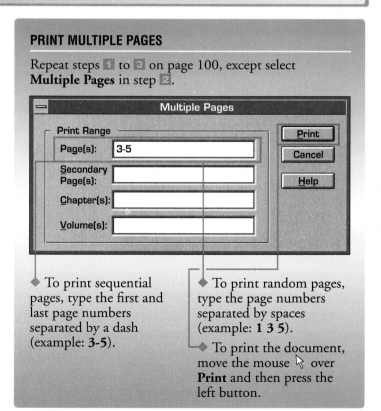

◆ To print sequential pages, type the first and last page numbers separated by a dash (example: **3-5**).

◆ To print random pages, type the page numbers separated by spaces (example: **1 3 5**).

◆ To print the document, move the mouse ⟍ over **Print** and then press the left button.

> You can use the Envelope feature to create and then print an envelope.

## Print an Envelope

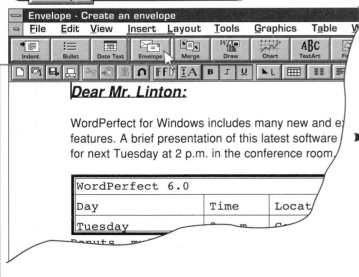

### Dear Mr. Linton:

WordPerfect for Windows includes many new and e[x] features. A brief presentation of this latest software for next Tuesday at 2 p.m. in the conference room.

| WordPerfect 6.0 | | |
|---|---|---|
| Day | Time | Locat |
| Tuesday | | C |

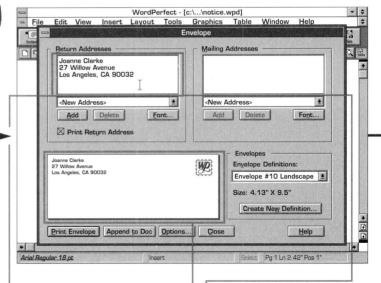

**1** Move the mouse � over ▣ and then press the left button.

◆ The **Envelope** dialog box appears.

**2** To print a return address on the envelope, move the mouse I over this area and then press the left button.

**3** Type the return address. Press **Enter** after you type each line of text.

◆ A sample of your envelope shows how the text will appear.

| Getting Started | Edit Your Documents | Save and Open Your Documents | Check Your Documents | Change Document View | Format Your Documents | Create a Table | **Print Your Documents** | Use Multiple Documents | Using Graphics | Merge Documents |

Print a Document
**Print an Envelope**

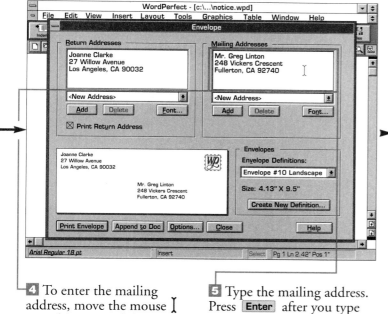

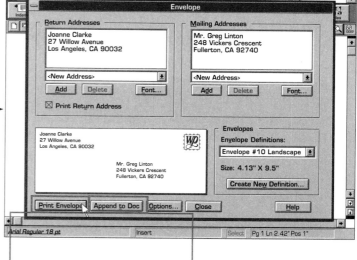

**4** To enter the mailing address, move the mouse I over this area and then press the left button.

*Note: A mailing address automatically appears in the **Mailing Addresses** area if WordPerfect finds one in the current document.*

**5** Type the mailing address. Press **Enter** after you type each line of text.

**6** To print the envelope, move the mouse ⌖ over **Print Envelope** and then press the left button.

♦ To add the envelope to the end of your document, move the mouse ⌖ over **Append to Doc** and then press the left button. This enables you to save and print the envelope with your document.

# CREATE A NEW DOCUMENT

# SWITCH BETWEEN DOCUMENTS

You can create a document to start a new letter, report or memo. WordPerfect enables you to have nine separate documents open at the same time.

## Create a New Document

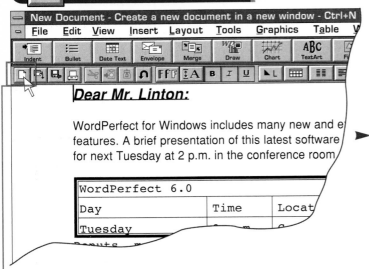

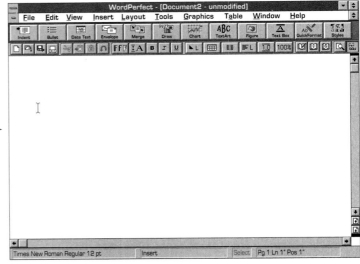

**1** Move the mouse ⌖ over ▢ and then press the left button.

◆ A new document appears.

*Note: The previous document is now hidden behind the new document.*

## CLOSE A DOCUMENT

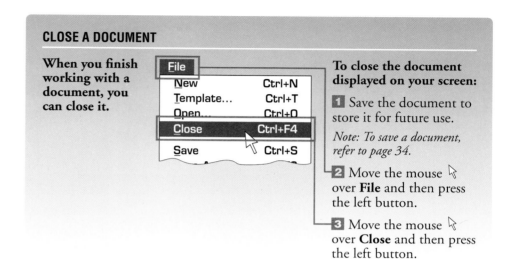

When you finish working with a document, you can close it.

**To close the document displayed on your screen:**

**1** Save the document to store it for future use.

*Note: To save a document, refer to page 34.*

**2** Move the mouse ⟨ over **File** and then press the left button.

**3** Move the mouse ⟨ over **Close** and then press the left button.

## Switch Between Documents

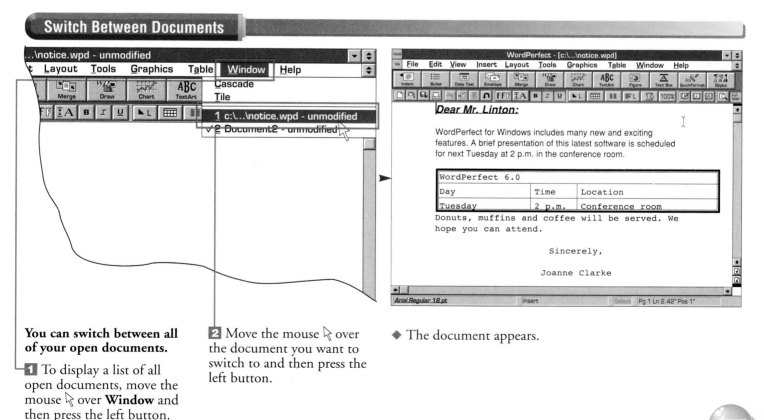

**You can switch between all of your open documents.**

**1** To display a list of all open documents, move the mouse ⟨ over **Window** and then press the left button.

**2** Move the mouse ⟨ over the document you want to switch to and then press the left button.

◆ The document appears.

# COPY OR MOVE TEXT
# BETWEEN DOCUMENTS

You can copy or move text from one document to another. This can save you time if you are working on a document and want to use text from another document.

## Copy or Move Text Between Documents

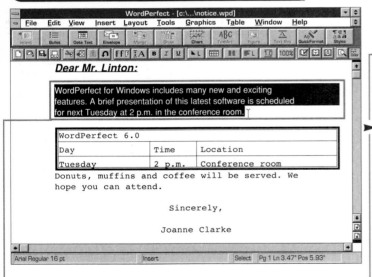

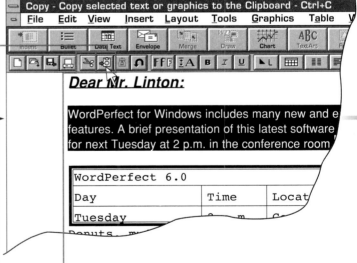

**1** Select the text you want to copy or move to another document.

*Note: To select text, refer to page 14.*

**2** To copy the text, move the mouse ⬡ over 🔲 and then press the left button. The selected text remains on your screen.

◆ To move the text, move the mouse ⬡ over ✂ and then press the left button. The selected text disappears from your screen.

| Getting Started | Edit Your Documents | Save and Open Your Documents | Check Your Documents | Change Document View | Format Your Documents | Create a Table | Print Your Documents | Use Multiple Documents | Using Graphics | Merge Documents |
|---|---|---|---|---|---|---|---|---|---|---|

Create a New Document
Switch Between Documents
**Copy or Move Text Between Documents**

## MOVE TEXT

When you **move** text, WordPerfect "cuts" the text and "pastes" it in a new location. The original text disappears.

## COPY TEXT

When you **copy** text, WordPerfect "copies" the text and "pastes" the copy in a new location. The original text remains in its place.

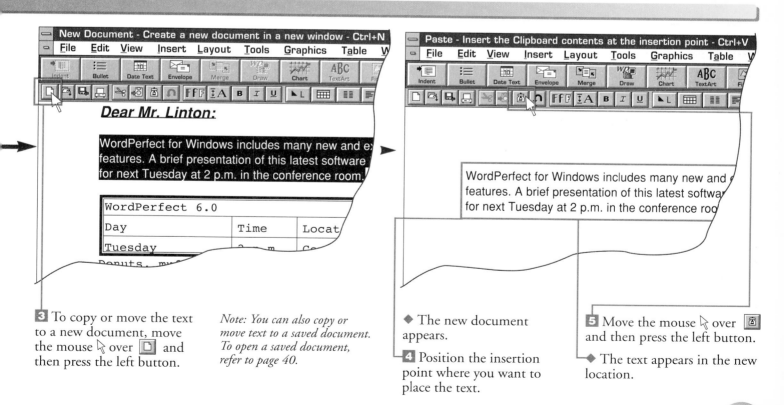

**3** To copy or move the text to a new document, move the mouse ⬚ over 🔲 and then press the left button.

*Note: You can also copy or move text to a saved document. To open a saved document, refer to page 40.*

◆ The new document appears.

**4** Position the insertion point where you want to place the text.

**5** Move the mouse ⬚ over 🔳 and then press the left button.

◆ The text appears in the new location.

# ADD A GRAPHICS IMAGE

You can make your document more attractive and interesting by adding a graphics image. WordPerfect provides over one hundred images that you can choose from.

**Add a Graphics Image to Your Document**

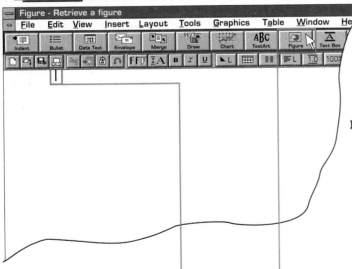

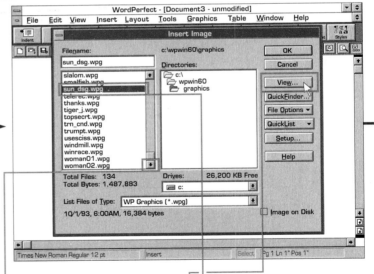

**This example adds a graphics image to a new document displayed in the Draft mode.**

*Note: To create a new document, refer to page 104. To change to the Draft mode, refer to page 54.*

**1** Position the insertion point where you want the image to appear.

**2** Move the mouse ⟍ over [Figure] and then press the left button.

◆ The **Insert Image** dialog box appears.

**3** To scroll through the list of available images, move the mouse ⟍ over the down arrow ⬇ and then press the left button.

**4** Move the mouse ⟍ over an image of interest (example: **sun_dsg.wpg**) and then press the left button.

**5** To preview the image, move the mouse ⟍ over **View** and then press the left button.

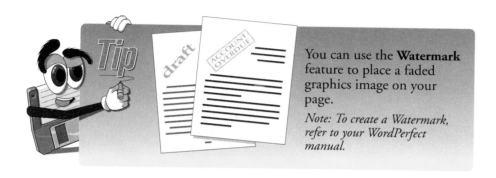

You can use the **Watermark** feature to place a faded graphics image on your page.

*Note: To create a Watermark, refer to your WordPerfect manual.*

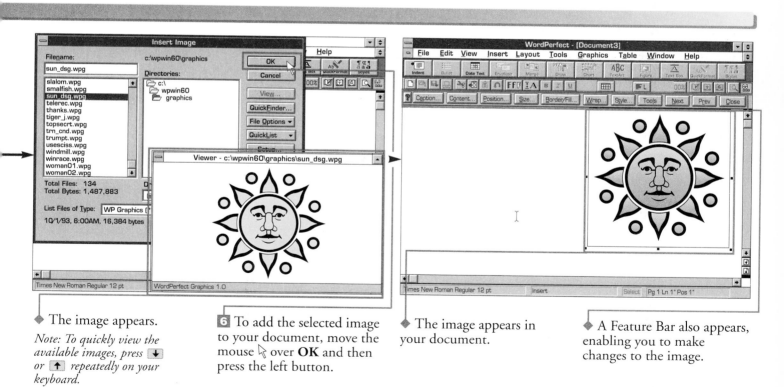

◆ The image appears.

*Note: To quickly view the available images, press ↓ or ↑ repeatedly on your keyboard.*

**6** To add the selected image to your document, move the mouse ⌀ over **OK** and then press the left button.

◆ The image appears in your document.

◆ A Feature Bar also appears, enabling you to make changes to the image.

You can move a graphics image to a new location in your document. You can also change its size.

## Move a Graphics Image

**1** Move the mouse I over the image you want to move.

**2** Press and hold down the left button as you drag the image to a new location.

◆ A dotted rectangular box indicates the new location.

**3** Release the button to move the image.

| Getting Started | Edit Your Documents | Save and Open Your Documents | Check Your Documents | Change Document View | Format Your Documents | Create a Table | Print Your Documents | Use Multiple Documents | **Using Graphics** | Merge Documents |

Add a Graphics Image
Move a Graphics Image
Size a Graphics Image

## DELETE A GRAPHICS IMAGE

**1** To select the graphics image you want to delete, move the mouse I over the image and then press the left button.

**2** Press Delete.

## Size a Graphics Image

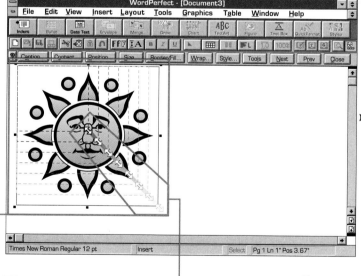

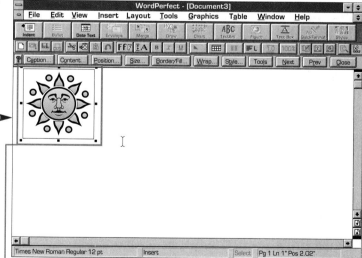

**1** To select the image you want to size, move the mouse I over the image and then press the left button.

◆ Squares (■) appear around the image.

**2** Move the mouse I over a square (■) and I changes to ↖.

**3** Press and hold down the left button as you drag the sides of the image to the desired size.

**4** Release the button to change the size of the image.

*Note: You can change the size of an image by dragging any square (■) around the image. A corner square will change the length and width of the image at the same time.*

111

You can use the Merge feature to create a letter and then have WordPerfect produce personalized copies for each person on your mailing list. To accomplish this task, you must create a Form and a Data file.

## Form File

A Form file contains the text that will appear in each letter. It also contains FIELD codes that tell WordPerfect where to insert the personalized information that changes from letter to letter.

## Data File

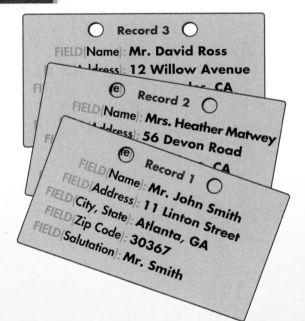

A Data file contains the information for each person you want to send the letter to (example: names, addresses).

The information for each person is called a **record**.

The information within each record is broken down into **fields**.

Getting
Started

Edit
Your
Documents

Save and
Open Your
Documents

Check
Your
Documents

Change
Document
View

Format
Your
Documents

Create
a Table

Print
Your
Documents

Use
Multiple
Documents

Using
Graphics

**Merge
Documents**

## Merged File

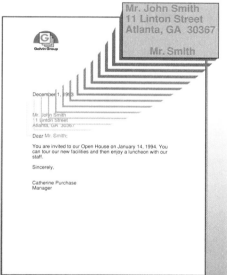
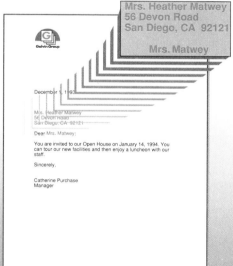

**This file is the result of merging the Form and Data files.**

**WordPerfect inserts the personalized information from the Data file into the Form file.**

# CREATE A DATA FILE

A Data file contains information for each person you want to send a letter to. This file may include information such as names and addresses.

## Create a Data File

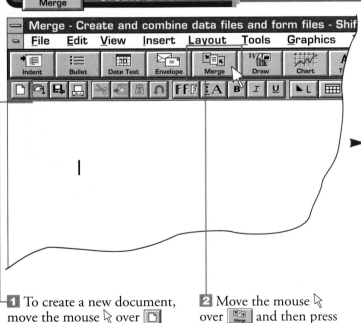

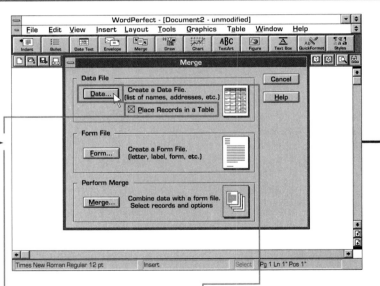

**1** To create a new document, move the mouse ⟋ over 🗋 and then press the left button.

**2** Move the mouse ⟋ over 📇 and then press the left button.

◆ The **Merge** dialog box appears.

**3** To place your information in a table, move the mouse ⟋ over **Place Records in a Table** and then press the left button (☐ becomes ☒).

**4** To create a data file, move the mouse ⟋ over **Data** and then press the left button.

| Getting Started | Edit Your Documents | Save and Open Your Documents | Check Your Documents | Change Document View | Format Your Documents | Create a Table | Print Your Documents | Use Multiple Documents | Using Graphics | **Merge Documents** |

Introduction
**Create a Data File**
Create a Form File
Merge Files

## FIELD NAMES

To create a data file, you must divide your information into categories and provide a term that describes each one. These terms are known as **field names**.

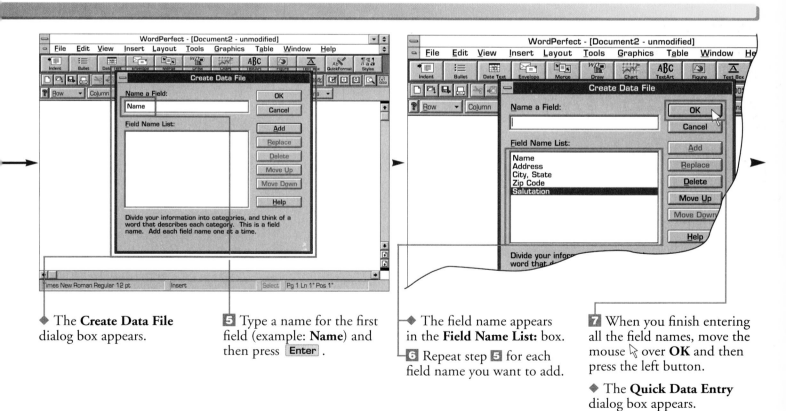

◆ The **Create Data File** dialog box appears.

**5** Type a name for the first field (example: **Name**) and then press **Enter**.

◆ The field name appears in the **Field Name List:** box.

**6** Repeat step **5** for each field name you want to add.

**7** When you finish entering all the field names, move the mouse over **OK** and then press the left button.

◆ The **Quick Data Entry** dialog box appears.

*Note: To continue creating the data file, refer to the next page.*

## Create a Data File (continued)

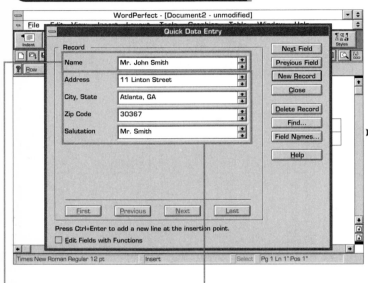

**8** Type the information that corresponds to the first field (example: **Mr. John Smith**).

**9** Press **Tab** to enter information into the next field.

**10** Repeat steps **8** and **9** until you finish typing all the information for the customer.

**11** To add new customer information, move the mouse ♀ over **New Record** and then press the left button.

**12** Repeat steps **8** to **11** for each customer.

**13** When you finish entering all your customer information, move the mouse ♀ over **Close** and then press the left button.

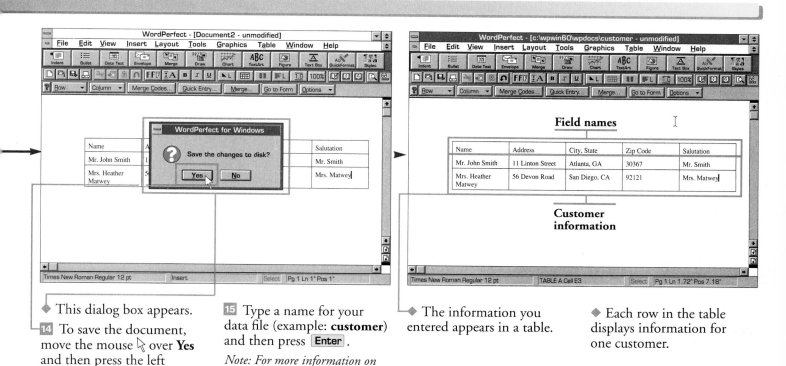

♦ This dialog box appears.

**14** To save the document, move the mouse ↳ over **Yes** and then press the left button.

♦ The **Save Data File As** dialog box appears.

**15** Type a name for your data file (example: **customer**) and then press **Enter**.

*Note: For more information on saving documents, refer to page 34.*

♦ The information you entered appears in a table.

♦ Each row in the table displays information for one customer.

---

## CHANGE CUSTOMER INFORMATION

If a customer's mailing address changes, you can edit the information displayed in the table.

**1** Move the mouse I over the information in the table you want to change and then press the left button.

**2** Move the mouse ↳ over Quick Entry... and then press the left button. The **Quick Data Entry** dialog box appears.

**3** Press **Tab** until you highlight the information you want to change.

**4** Type the new information.

**5** Repeat steps **3** and **4** until you finish making the changes.

**6** Move the mouse ↳ over Close and then press the left button.

# CREATE A FORM FILE

A Form file contains the text that will appear in each letter. It also contains codes that tell WordPerfect where to insert the information from the Data file.

## Create a Form File

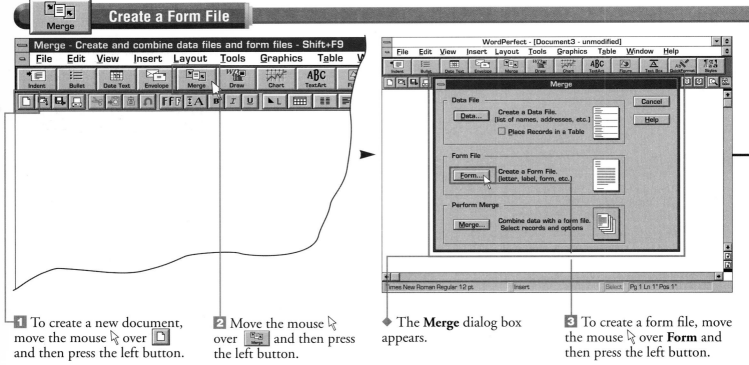

**1** To create a new document, move the mouse ░ over 🗋 and then press the left button.

**2** Move the mouse ░ over ⬚ and then press the left button.

◆ The **Merge** dialog box appears.

**3** To create a form file, move the mouse ░ over **Form** and then press the left button.

Getting Started | Edit Your Documents | Save and Open Your Documents | Check Your Documents | Change Document View | Format Your Documents | Create a Table | Print Your Documents | Use Multiple Documents | Using Graphics | **Merge Documents**

Introduction
Create a Data File
**Create a Form File**
Merge Files

# IMPORTANT!

◆ To display the example below more clearly, the design and size of the text were changed.

*Note: To change the design and size of text, refer to page 66.*

| Initial or default font | New font |
|---|---|
| Times New Roman 12 point ► | **Arial 16 point** |

◆ To work faster in WordPerfect, display the document in the Draft mode.

*Note: To change modes, refer to page 54.*

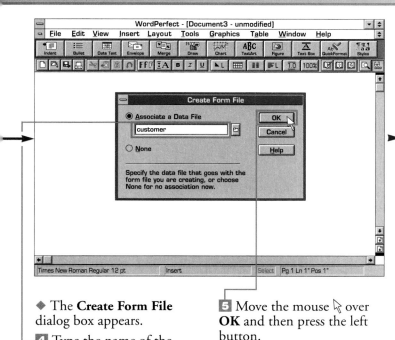

◆ The **Create Form File** dialog box appears.

**4** Type the name of the data file you want to associate with the form file you are creating (example: **customer**).

**5** Move the mouse ↳ over **OK** and then press the left button.

**6** Begin typing the letter as you would any WordPerfect document.

*Note: To continue creating the form file, refer to the next page.*

119

## Create a Form File (continued)

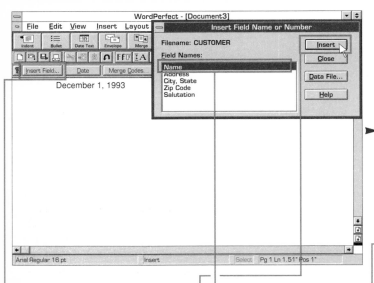

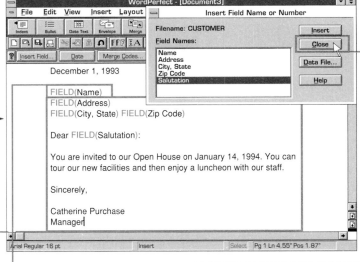

**7** When you reach the part of the letter where you want to insert information from the data file, move the mouse over **Insert Field** and then press the left button.

**8** Move the mouse over the field name you want to insert (example: **Name**) and then press the left button.

**9** Move the mouse over **Insert** and then press the left button.

◆ A **FIELD** code appears on your screen.

**10** Continue typing the letter, repeating steps **8** and **9** for each field you want to insert.

*Note: To start a new line, press* **Enter** *.*

**11** When you finish entering all the field names, move the mouse over **Close** and then press the left button.

**12** Save the document to store it for future use. In this example, the document was named **letter.wpd**.

*Note: To save a document, refer to page 34.*

◆ When you merge the data and form files, the information from the data file replaces the codes displayed in your document.

| Getting Started | Edit Your Documents | Save and Open Your Documents | Check Your Documents | Change Document View | Format Your Documents | Create a Table | Print Your Documents | Use Multiple Documents | Using Graphics | **Merge Documents** |
|---|---|---|---|---|---|---|---|---|---|---|

Introduction
Create a Data File
**Create a Form File**
Merge Files

## USING MERGE TO CREATE ENVELOPES

**You can create an envelope for every customer in your data file.**

**1** Perform steps **1** to **5** on pages 118 and 119.

**2** Move the mouse ⌖ over 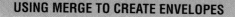 and then press the left button. The **Envelope** dialog box appears.

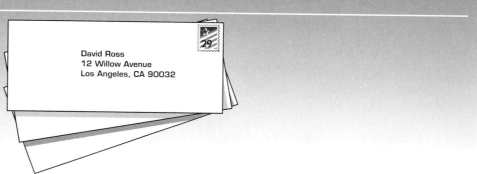

David Ross
12 Willow Avenue
Los Angeles, CA 90032

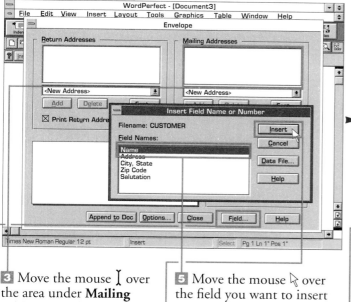

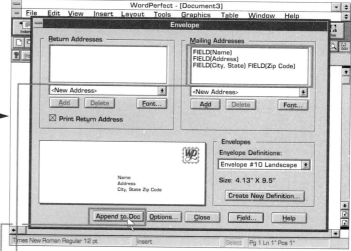

**3** Move the mouse I over the area under **Mailing Addresses** and then press the left button.

**4** Move the mouse ⌖ over **Field** and then press the left button.

**5** Move the mouse ⌖ over the field you want to insert (example: **Name**) and then press the left button.

**6** Move the mouse ⌖ over **Insert** and then press the left button.

**7** To insert the next field on the following line, press **Enter**.

*Note: To insert the next field on the same line, press the **Spacebar**.*

**8** Repeat steps **4** to **6** for each field you want to insert.

**9** Move the mouse ⌖ over **Append to Doc** and then press the left button.

**10** Save the document.

*Note: To save the document, refer to page 34.*

◆ You have created a form file. To create an envelope for every customer, you must merge this form file with a data file (example: **customer**). To merge files, refer to the next page.

121

# MERGE FILES

You can combine a Form and Data file to create a personalized letter for several people.

---

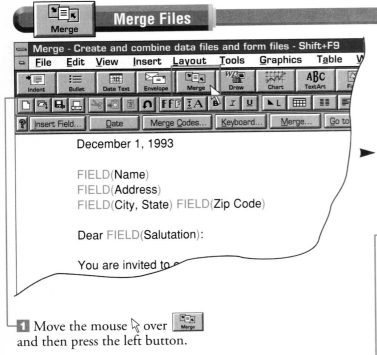

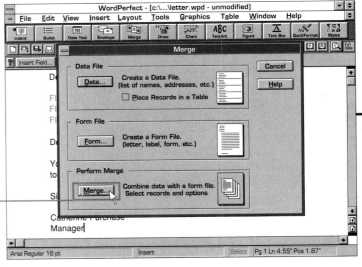

**1** Move the mouse ⌖ over [Merge] and then press the left button.

◆ The **Merge** dialog box appears.

**2** Move the mouse ⌖ over **Merge** and then press the left button.

◆ The **Perform Merge** dialog box appears.

◆ To conserve hard disk space, do not save the merged document after you print it. You can easily recreate this document by repeating steps **1** to **5** below.

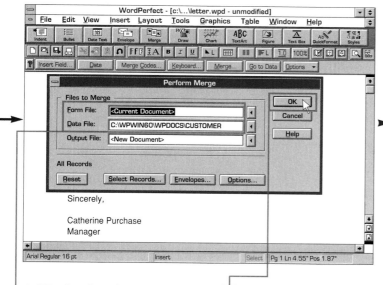

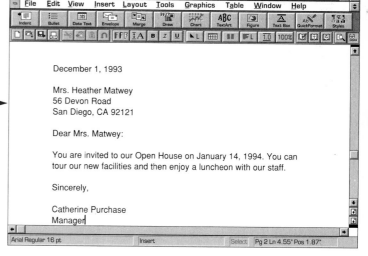

◆ WordPerfect displays the names of the files it will merge.

**3** If this dialog box does not display the correct names of the files you want to merge, press Tab until you highlight the filename you want to change and then type the correct name.

**4** Move the mouse over **OK** and then press the left button.

◆ The form and data files are merged.

**5** Press PageUp to view the letters to ensure no errors have occurred.

◆ You can edit and print this document as you would any WordPerfect document.

# INDEX